ESG EXPLORED

Environmental, Social and Governance reporting for small businesses in Australia

by

DR JOHN ROCHECOUSTE AND SARAH DELAHUNTY

A catalogue record for this book is available from the National Library of Australia

Publisher:
Australian Self Publishing Group, Pty. Ltd/Inspiring Publishers
PO Box 159, Calwell, ACT 2905
Australia. Phone: 61-(0) 2 6291-2904
http://australianselfpublishinggroup.com

Member of the:
Australian Publishers Association,
International Book Publishing Association,
The Small Press Network

National Library of Australia Cataloguing-in-Publication entry

Author: Dr John Rochecouste and Sarah Delahunty

Title: **ESG EXPLORED: Environmental Social Governance**

Genre: non-fiction, business

ISBN: 978-1-923087-34-7 (Print)

ISBN: 978-1-923087-33-0 (ePub2)

Contents

Author Bios

Dr John Rochecouste is a current sustainability consultant to rural industries and a co-founder of ESG Explored. He holds a doctorate on climate change impacts, a masters on business and environment and a degree in agricultural science. He has published several journal papers and book chapters on Conservation Agriculture. He has a career spanning 40 years in the agricultural and environmental sector working both in the corporate and government sector. Now retired, he still maintains an active role in supporting business sustainability.

Sarah Delahunty has worked as a Stakeholder Engagement and Corporate Partnership professional over many years and across a variety of industries. Sarah has seen the evolution of ESG from the 'nice to have' social licence to operate to the essential business agency lens of ESG. Identifying the changing ways stakeholders wanted to receive information and the confusion around how organisations could collect and report the information. Sarah started ESG Explored in early 2022 as a way to provide practical advice and information.

Acknowledgements

We would like to especially thank Madalyn Grant and Emma McTaggart for their support and significant contributions. Also, to all our wonderful industry experts who shared their knowledge on the ESG Explored podcasts.

Introduction

This book is for small to medium enterprises and is designed to help you navigate the world of Environmental, Social and corporate Governance (ESG). As an environmental sustainability scientist and along with my co-author a stakeholder engagement professional, it became obvious to us that small business had a lot of questions about what ESG was. Clearly, the big end of town was well organised to manage ESG but there was a clear knowledge gap at the level of small to medium enterprises. To fill this gap, we felt a clear easy to read book might be the answer. We decided it should be formatted as a conversation, sharing the wisdom of the many people we have talked to over time. The subject is big, but not overwhelming, and there is a level of common sense to the process.

We wanted this book to help the thousands of small businesses that may not have a public relations department on staff. It can also be useful to middle management to understand why boards are so focussed on ESG. It will give you some common-sense strategies to avoid falling into those public relations holes in the first place. Avoiding the hole is a far cheaper option than trying to dig yourself out; and in some cases, the hole may just be too big to get out of! As the owner or manager of a business, this is going to demand a bit of work rethinking the way you look at your business. There are no set recipes in this book; it is simply a conversation about ideas, experiences, and lessons that others are willing to share. We will begin by attempting to answer the many questions that are often raised by small business about ESG. We will also try to be pragmatic about what is possible and what is not when considering ESG.

OK, so what is ESG?

A business is an entity on paper, it does not have a social conscience, it is the humans in the business who provide the conscience. ESG reporting is the details that you as the owner and manager provide about how the business is addressing its relationship to society and the environment. There is no legal requirement for ESG reporting beyond the existing legal instruments, it should be a clear statement of your action to support a fair-minded process for your customers or investors. Certainly, in some cases, large corporations or governments will require a level of action from you as a supplier to manage their own ESG requirements. You will most likely be asked about how you are managing your sustainability obligation as part of the larger supply chain. You may not be under additional legal obligation, but you may be subject to a level of competitive pressure. Businesses are rarely rewarded for doing the right thing, but you are more likely to lose business if you cannot meet customer requirements. ESG should also be considered as more than a framework for action, it requires us to actually 'think' differently. It is less about ticking a compliance box and more about putting some thought into engineering an equitable future for 8 billion people.

In the nineties, reporting largely focused on corporate social responsibility. Increasingly, investors and customers wanted to better understand both the environmental and social impact of business. They felt it should cover not only your business region of operation but the upstream impact of the goods and services you deliver. Who made the goods you are selling? How did they make this? Was there serious environmental damage in producing these goods? Corporate behaviour here or overseas that came to light as damaging the environment or was socially unacceptable became a risk to the business. Moreover, the reporting for big business provided investors a clearer picture of their business risk position. The same risk that applies to big business also applies to you as a small business. Admittedly, not every business is sold on the value of ESG, but even if only 30 percent of your customers or investors have concerns about your practices, that is a sizeable chunk of your resources if they should walk away.

ESG is about amplifying the consideration of the environment when compared to the previous social responsibility expected of businesses. The community is asking business to outline truthfully what it is doing for people and the environment. In the end, it is the millions of customers, investors, employees, and lenders who will actually determine if the concept of ESG is an aberration or something they actually do care about. In our experience, most companies are not willing to risk being left behind by their competitors, hence why so many are making the change to include ESG as part of doing business.

ESG is all about taking stock of your business via a 360-degree view for possible risks. It is the totality of the process that is becoming increasingly important. Just for a moment, forget about external compliance and focus on what you do as a business - who are you and what do you stand for? What is your purpose?

The move beyond corporate social responsibility has been driven largely by the major fund managers in response to the demand of their clients. For investors it is just as important for a business to look after both its staff, its community, and the broader environment. It cannot focus on just one at the expense of the other. Investors do not see that as being sustainable.

In summary what ESG is asking of you as the conscience of the business is: what are you doing for our community? and what are you doing for our environment?

Why is ESG important?

Let's consider one of the most important ingredients of business, something that is more important than capital. The one thing your business cannot do without – trust! Stephen Covey wrote that "low trust is the greatest cost in life and in organizations"[1]. It can increase your business to ever greater heights or risk losing it altogether. Given its importance, how much effort do you put into managing it? There are several areas that trust applies and these include staff, suppliers, customers, government, and the broader public.

CASE EXAMPLE

A current example regarding trust is media reports about the role of international accounting firm PwC, once known as Pricewaterhouse Coopers, a global brand operating internationally with over 300,000 employees. It branded itself a few years ago with the word "trust" front and centre of its marketing campaign. PwC, as one of the four big accounting firms, has been a major beneficiary of the government consultancy boom in Australia. The Australian government had asked PwC tax expert Peter Collins to help it design laws to better tax multinational companies, due to a number of large companies, particularly tech giants, shifting profits from higher-taxing countries like Australia to others like The Netherlands and Singapore with lower tax rates. Despite the confidentiality agreement in place, Peter Collins shared the confidential knowledge within PwC and with their overseas partners, helping the firm create a system for those companies to avoid paying the new taxes. The company used this privileged information to make money and win new clients; it was reported that PwC made at least $2.5 million in fees from the deception – a rather small amount relative to their 50-billion-dollar revenues in 2022. However, this breach of trust by a few senior employees had

---

[1] Covey, S.M.R. & Merrill, R.R., 2008. *The Speed of Trust – the one thing that changes everything.* Free Press, Simon & Schuster, Inc. New York

> significant consequences for the business, not only in Australia but internationally. The story made international headlines leaving the brand in serious jeopardy. The fallout was the Australian CEO and a number of senior employees resigned. With potential further legal action, the suggestion is that this breach of trust will have ramifications for a long time to come – and likely not only for PwC.

When considering ESG reporting, it's worth reflecting on how your business operates, what is it offering, and how does it do that. The 'how' is what we will be most concerned about when considering ESG. Let's start with some basics.

Staff are key to most businesses, but as individuals they have their own moral code that they bring to work. This is applied as part of their job, regardless of whether or not they mean to, and regardless of whether you are there to supervise or not. If there is one thing the outbreak of COVID-19 has demonstrated is how strong some people feel about life outside their job. Think of people who pointedly refuse to wear masks regardless of legal directives or people who have left their secure job to pursue a career elsewhere. We have also seen great loyalty by staff to their workplace, coming in to work without pay.

The supplier relationship is also critical, especially in times of shortages and stress. Small businesses often have a limited buffer of stock, so in times of shortages not having that stock is going to seriously impact profit. This doesn't just apply to goods; it can also be subcontractors. The building industry in 2020's Australia has been plagued with shortages and many jobs simply could not be completed. This is not to mention the legacy of having dissatisfied customers because builders could not supply the goods and services they committed to. We can ask, what could they have done about this? We will consider some strategies that can improve that relationship, particularly with the more critical suppliers. We will analyse how the winners and losers played their strategies during shortages.

Another key part of the business is the customer. They pay your bills and provide you a living. If they walk away, you are toast, it's as simple as that. Customers can seem a bit fickle at times, sensitive about how you should treat them and not always up-front about how they feel about you. Not all customers feel comfortable complaining or having a confrontation so it may seem like a 50:50 bet if they will come back. The product-price point is certainly important but so is the trust they need to have in your business. If they tend to think you are not being entirely honest with them, or your values are radically different to theirs, they may well take up an alternative option. It can make the difference between you and a competitor. ESG is a lot about being honest and engendering trust in your customers that you are a responsible corporate citizen.

Finally, there is public sentiment. While the theme of the movie 'The Wolf of Wall Street' might have characterised the idea of greed is good, it should also be remembered that humans are communal by nature and doing members of the community a bad deed will not go unpunished. Even if people are not your direct customer, they can impact your business. It's worth remembering that businesses are part of a commercial ecosystem and social milieu. Staff at a key supplier, a regulator, or subcontractor you depend on are all part of a community that may not be your direct customer but impact your business in some way. If they are unhappy about the way you do business, they can possibly delay services or payment and you would have no way of knowing about this. Put succinctly, be mindful of who you choose to annoy.

Being open, fair minded, and truthful in your dealings is a clear requirement to engendering trust. So, when reporting how you manage your business, transparency about how you treat the people, and the environment is important.

Sustainable Development Goals

The question most people have is, how do you know what you should be looking for when considering implementing an ESG framework for your business? Is there a list? Well actually there is, and the best place to start is to look up the 17 United Nation's Sustainable Development Goals[2]. There you will find a menu that lists all the 17 things you should be taking account of. You will also find sub-menus under each goal about actions you can take. The sub-menus will also list global targets and indicators. There is a large swath of information to explore.

Some will have minimal relevance and might be hard for you to engage with, whilst others will be highly relevant. In some ways, as part of a supply chain, there is a quite a bit you can do as a buyer of inputs by informing yourself about where and how the things you purchase are made. Let's say you have a corporate quote for 100 branded shirts at $15 per shirt, and another quote that's $19 per shirt. Saving yourself $400 isn't much in the scheme of things, but as a business you are discerning where you spend and where you save. However, let's look at what that $400 is costing you ethically and socially. Do you know the provenance of these items? If the cheaper item is later associated with the use of slave labour or discovered to be environmentally exploitive, it will certainly cost you more than $400.

You can start to unpick the matters by asking yourself 'what impact or damage is my business having on the community around me based on what I hear is important to the community?' We will cover this in more detail in the 'Social' section.

For now, the easiest way to map your ESG requirement is to consider what part of the Sustainable Development Goals might apply and the level of relevance it has to your business, either directly or via your supply chain. You will notice that climate action is only one of those goals, despite it taking on greater focus for many businesses at the

---

[2] https://sdgs.un.org/goals

moment. A great deal of what you can do is to ensure your inputs are coming from a sustainable reputable source. Recently, the car manufacturer Volkswagen was asked about its investment in China's western region of Xinjiang under new German Government supply chain rules targeting human rights violations. The company stresses that it does not use any slave labour in its factory and has audited some of its suppliers. This is the type of pressures some of these big brands such as Adidas, Puma, BMW, Bosch, and Siemens are under in reporting on their due diligence to the German Government. This is set to become commonplace across the developed world after COP 27.

In an interview with Steve Greenwood, the CEO of Queensland Futures Institute, he considers that his members are keenly aware of the reputational issues around ESG[3]. Reputational risk for large corporates is everything. It is subsequently a big focus for his members, and it would be fair to say that "there's a lot of questions at a board level around standards and compliance." He comments that a lot of organisations can already demonstrate that they're meeting some of those ESG goals. This is an important consideration, and suggests that:

> 'One of the biggest things, and I think one of the things that is part of the ESG discussion, is that the world we live in, particularly focusing on Australia and Queensland, we actually are one of the wealthiest, most highly advanced nations in the world. There's no question, so a lot of our core systems and procedures are very sophisticated. From my point of view, we're not starting from ground zero. A lot of our societal systems, our legal requirements for instance, our environmental requirements is for me quite sophisticated. Therefore, we are already partly there through that legislation, through compliance with a lot of those existing laws and societal expectations.'

---

[3]Greenwood, S. 2022. Interview with authors on ESG Explored podcast Episode 2 October 2022.

This is certainly worth considering – that under Australian laws we are already meeting a lot of our social obligations. But perhaps it is not something we should become too complacent about. We can point to poor behaviour by large corporations because they are more likely to come under media scrutiny at the global level, but we each in our own way must make ethical decisions about the business we are responsible for or work in.

How important is ESG to SMEs?

Given, you are not a large corporation. We get that, but ESG still applies in that customers have a choice. This means a competitor down the road may be promoting themselves as more environmentally friendly, or more involved in supporting community sport, or have more happy, friendly staff. Whatever it is, price is not the only factor that attracts customers; prestige and corporate purpose are also strong drivers for customers.

The other point worth considering is that you deal with other businesses as part of a supply chain. Those businesses may have made a commitment to reducing their emissions, be more socially conscious, or reducing their level of waste. You then become part of their commitment. If you wrap your products to be delivered in non-biodegradable plastic, you are now affecting their waste stream and so it goes. You are effectively transferring an issue downstream and at some point, you might expect to be questioned on this.

Let's consider events such as the 2032 Brisbane Olympic games, for example. Barton Green, CEO of the committee for Brisbane, indicated that in his experience, his members are in fact mostly SMEs, and they are increasingly looking at investing in products that are not your traditional shopping centres or commercial buildings or agricultural land[4]. They are supportive of trying things like social and affordable housing

[4]Green, B. 2022. Interview with authors on ESG Explored podcast Episode 7 November 2022

being built with a view that there can still be a guaranteed long term steady return.

> 'It might be a bit different to others, but it's the social return on investment that is now becoming a critical part of some of these conversations, which fits beautifully into the ESG space. I'll go back to the Olympics and Paralympics because they're a good case study then with respect to supply chain on the contract that the city has to its suppliers for the Brisbane 2032 games. The contract that we have with the International Olympic Committee requires a number of significant commitments in the space we're talking about that we have a 'climate positive games', and that we have a circular economy game.'

What is the environment part in ESG referring to?

All entities have a footprint. This is the space you occupy in the supply chain and the impact you have downstream. The most obvious ones are energy use, pollution, and waste generation. You cannot 'not' have a footprint, only that you might want to not make it bigger than it needs to be. This can lead to some of the more subtle areas of environmental impacts.

What is becoming increasingly apparent to consumers is a lot of packaging which ends up in landfill is more about advertising and selling set volumes than the safe or secure transportation of products. According to the Australian Bureau of Statistics 2020, Australia produces about 76 million tonnes of waste each year and only about half is recycled[5]. When you get further into the details it becomes a horrifying story of waste, often from poor commercial design. Packaging that has mixed plastic/paper/foams etc cannot be easily recycled so they are

---

[5]Australian Bureau of Statistics 2020 - Waste generation, management and economic response by industry and household in alignment with System of Environmental-Economic Accounts (SEEA). Waste Account, Australia, Experimental Estimates Latest release - Reference period 2018-19 financial year.

destined for landfill. Increasingly business will become responsible for the waste stream they produce. This is happening slowly, so some businesses are gearing up for the change, but many are completely ignoring the likelihood of it ever happening.

In the section on environment, we will look more closely at the impact of business on the planet. Ecological economics tells us that our impact on the planet's natural resources, something that we rely on, has become so big that we can no longer assume that it will continue to support humanity in the way it did two centuries ago. There is a mental gap between knowing 'we do not have another planet' and actually doing something here and now to maintain this one.

What does social in ESG refer to?

Social refers to your impact on the community. The provision of a living wage is probably one of the more commonly referred-to goals by the United Nations because of its impact on many other things. There is also a need for a more proactive stance on gender, race, and religious discrimination. In Australia most of these fundamental issues are legislated. However Australian businesses and consumers do purchase a great deal from countries that have no such laws. Businesses are also responsible to fairly treat their staff and ensure the safety of staff, customers, and the community.

The social impact a business has beyond its legal obligation is nuanced; hence why it is not always easy to manage. For example, the Australian Government's 'Respect at Work' Bill 2022 places a positive duty on all employers to implement measures to prevent sexual harassment. What constitutes sexual harassment is outlined but it is unlikely most employees would be aware of the detail of where a 'it's just a joke' becomes harassment. Rather than trying to learn the fine legal lines, we suggest you develop a formal cultural expectation of respect within the workplace. Make it explicit and highly visible, not simply implicit.

Cultural norms are important because we live and work in a complex world where there are inherent risks for misunderstanding. In 2021 the Australian High Court ruled that media companies could be liable for defamatory comments made by readers on their Facebook posts. The ruling extended beyond Facebook. The court case only concerned Facebook, but the decision has implications for other social media platforms your organisation may be using if you do not vet comments to be posted. It can be argued that the whole reason for social media is to be immediately responsive without everything being formally vetted such as in a 'press release.' The issue with social media for businesses is exactly that it is 'immediate' and provides less room for reflection. The immediacy of the moment can on occasion allow the writer to vent without considering the impact – not unlike having a private conversation near a hot microphone. Do we really need to outline examples? Probably not! You only have to do a search for 'social media gaffes' for a list of sometimes hilarious to cringeworthy comments. A small diversion to the web at this point is okay to refresh your memory of some of the more fascinating 'what were they thinking?' moments.

This need for immediacy does present a risk where employees have access to comment on your platform and are therefore seen to be acting on behalf of the business or where they may use their personal social media but are known as your employee. Some have legal risks; other circumstances have reputational risks.

Your social responsibility covers a wide range of issues that deal with staff, customers, people in community, and even domestic animals you are responsible for. Getting this wrong can have serious impact on your business reputation. We cover this in more detail in the social chapter.

Why is governance as part of ESG important?

Governance is the foundation of your reputation. It's easy to fall into a casual way of doing things to save time and sparing yourself the pedantic boring processes that it may require. We share your pain. Just before you ask yourself, 'Does it really matter if the details are not recorded?' Well, yes it does. In the rush to get things done, missing the details can have important consequences. Governance is about having the framework that collects the information to justly defend your action. Mostly you won't need it, until you actually desperately need it, at which point it'll be too late to go back and get it. It's insurance for maintaining trust. Let's say you made an important claim based on general executive information given to you; but what happens if you are challenged, and you dig down to find the evidence doesn't support it? At best embarrassment, at worst, expensive liability.

It's common knowledge that success is everybody's child, but mistakes are orphans. Without a method for having transparency and people signing off on responsibility, no one will take credit for wrongdoing. The person who ends up carrying the liability may well be the innocent party, or you as the owner of the business. It's also not just a matter for large organisations, the risks are just as real for small business, maybe more so. Small businesses often operate with less processes and there is a more casual attitude to decision making. It is small so everybody knows what's going on, but this can also lead to complacency. The probability of issues of note arising are very low, but when it happens the consequences can be high.

How do you report on ESG?

The argument around this is based on the 'what are you supposed to report on?' If it was mandatory then there would be a form to fill out, but it's not, so the uncertainty means everyone has a different opinion about what's important. The reality is you get to choose what you feel is important to your investors, customers, and suppliers. Businesses are so varied it doesn't seem practical to have a one size fits all approach. The people who keep you in business will tell you what's important to them in continuing to be a customer. A lot of large corporates that have the dollars will monitor what the customer cares about and responds to those findings. We see this with banks, fast food chains, and car manufacturers. They know if they don't, their competitors might take market share off them or worse, make them irrelevant.

There is no set reporting method to ESG, but there are fundamentals. Carbon emissions are getting the most attention at the moment. However next year, it could be something else. The challenge is to be aware of your customer sentiment, and how to get the internal figures you need to maintain an agile response. Right now, you may be thinking more about climate change impacts around emissions and not be prepared to respond to your plastic use. Sentiments can change quickly as we saw with the sudden removal of plastic drinking straws in Australia following the television show "The War on Waste", hence the need to have a more structured approach to know how to collect the information you need and have alternative options in place.

Pay particular attention to any public statements you make in advertising. Ask yourself, can you back this up with detailed facts? If you have any doubt, don't do it. Don't make the statement. You are first of all gathering evidence and reporting back to yourself. This should be happening well before you go and tell the world what you are doing to be a good corporate citizen.

The structure of the information you collect on how your business is impacting the United Nations Development Goals is what you need to report. You don't have to do it all at once pick the most relevant ones first.

What Is the role of impact when considering ESG?

Impact is the flow-on effects of your action. It can be hard to measure, but even a qualitative understanding is a good start. Most impacts are small; major ones tend to come under some form of legislation. But even these small impacts, when reduced, can collectively make a difference. If as an individual we use tap water instead of bottled water when it's available, then that is one less plastic bottle in the waste stream. If we start to all do this collectively, it reduces demand and puts pressure on business and organisations to supply the alternative to plastic bottled water.

Impact can be reactive or proactive. For example, if demand for a product drops, you react by changing your supply options. In this instant you are reacting to market trends. However, a reactive strategy means you have to be agile. This doesn't suit the larger capital items that needs to deliver for decades. Capital expenditure requires you to think more proactively to avoid stranded assets. It's a no-brainer that those with energy assets would need to consider the push for electrification. You certainly don't have to be the first in the market, but you would best not be the last or ignore it altogether. It's quite obvious that you need to consider the depreciated value of any asset class. In some cases, the residual value may be a great deal less than you might think. Diesel passenger cars being the most evident example, less affected is commercial diesel vehicles with limited alternatives. Even where local sales might hold up in the short term, a global shift can very quickly affect the supply of parts. There is a cascading effect such as insurance and repair costs that can continue the decline in demand. Impacts are also tied to global events and, presently, there are no examples more obvious than the COVID-19 pandemic and now the war in Ukraine and its impact on prices and supply.

In terms of an ESG framework, impact is more directly related to your actions as a business. It can be measured in dollars such as your energy bill or in sentiment such as a drop in customer satisfaction. It can also affect your cost of production and staff satisfaction. Although hard to measure, asking the question helps to frame your thinking and consider 'how might I be able to measure this for the business?' Awareness is key.

Why is greenwashing a thing?

Putting the prefix 'Eco' or 'Bio' in front of a product doesn't make it environmentally sustainable. At this point it is simply an implied term, but this is only one step away from making a product statement that could end up in the category of being misleading.

Increasingly the buying public are getting wise to possible misrepresentation of this type of labelling and regulators are gradually stepping in to certify product registrations and labels. In many countries, registering a trademark comprising the word elements 'Eco' or 'Bio' requires the applicant to have an approval from an authorized body or state authority that any such trademark is indeed "ecological" or "biological".

Simply making vague statements that cannot be properly verified is greenwashing and it is coming under increasing scrutiny by authorities. As well as regulatory scrutiny, it is also being challenged by those who are putting significant resources and effort into actually being sustainable.

In March 2023, the Australian Competition & Consumer commission (ACCC) published its report on *Greenwashing by Businesses in Australia* and has announced a crackdown on greenwashing. As a result, the watchdog announced it would step up its probe of companies' environmental claims after an initial sweep of 247 businesses or brands across eight sectors found 57% had made misleading statements ranging from overstating climate action to developing their own certification schemes.

The report is worth the read. It indicates that some businesses are:

- Using vague or unclear environmental claims
- Not providing sufficient evidence for their claims
- Setting environmental goals without clear plans
- Using third-party certification and symbols in a confusing way.

Why is the ACCC pursuing this type of advertising? They outline more consumers are now relying on sustainability claims to make purchasing decisions, but that consumers cannot readily verify the accuracy of a business' environmental credentials and must trust the claims or impressions made.

The logic is that environmental or sustainability claims will only help consumers make informed purchasing decisions if the claims are clear, are not misleading, and do not omit relevant information. A misleading, meaningless, or unclear claim breaches consumer trust and hurts confidence in both the claim itself and sustainability claims in general.

They also recognise there is a cost to putting sustainability in place and it is unfair on those who have done the right thing. Being caught greenwashing has significant reputational risk, so it is worth doing your due diligence on the validity of a claim before someone else does it for you.

What do PR people do and why do organisations have them?

We mention Public Relations (PR) people in the ESG context because most small businesses don't have one in-house or hire them. The public relations job is to have a helicopter view looking across the community landscape and gauging the public (customer) mood on certain issues; testing public reactions, and factoring all of that into responses of the moment or future strategy. Although they are rarely hired by small businesses, we usually find small businesses have someone within the business who takes on this role in an informal way.

In times of great change, PR skills are very valuable and should be fostered. Corporations and political parties pay them to be close to the decision-makers for very good reason. They provide an external view that supports both tactical and strategic planning. Implementing an ESG framework requires a level of social cognitive skill and the resources to support it. It's not uncommon for the business owner or manager to do it as part of their job, but when changes are in flux, they can miss things simply because they have too much else to do.

The main reason to raise this point of public relations stems from the misconception that managing the ESG issue is often seen as an environmental engineering issue and misses the wider implications of social and governance. If we go back to reviewing the UN sustainability goals, we will see it's wide, very wide. Therefore, the strategic skill set to work on it must likewise be very wide. Someone managing ESG needs to have some capability around the technical, social, and process function of the organisation, without having to be the subject matter expert in any of those field. We do not yet have specialist ESG staff because our educational institutions are mostly based around specialisation and lack interdisciplinary education.

Public sentiment

There is not one public sentiment. It varies through all sorts of parameters: geography, age, gender, or socio-economic levels as just a few. The key for businesses is how to determine the ones to be mindful of, and the ones you can safely ignore. Most businesses attempt to stay neutral on controversial issues, but it is important to be aware of the shifts that can change the way you do business. Having a digital presence, or cashless facilities are some of those changes. Like having a social media presence, it may not be for everyone, but it will be for some businesses more than others.

Public sentiment, in our opinion, is shifting towards a greater demand from corporate Australia to demonstrate responsibility for planet and people. This is not just a younger generational trend but a broader demand for transparency in the wake of significant corporate failures of responsibility in areas of finance and environment. The pushback against globalisation is in part due to corporate failures like Enron (2001), Lehmann brothers (2008), General Motors (2009), Chrysler (2009), and more recently the crypto currency exchange FTX (2022 possibly valued at $32billion) which is still ongoing. This is all someone's money or life savings. Those collapses and many others have personally impacted people across all walks of life and increased the level of public insecurity.

But it's not just finance. Governments are becoming wary of being entirely dependent on overseas for the manufacture of critical commodities following the COVID-19 pandemic and now a war in Europe. As a consequence, investors (all of us in some way through superannuation) across the board are demanding greater transparency, not just in financial management but what are the sustainability risks that these companies face. This in turn is cascading down the supply chain placing greater demand on smaller suppliers of goods and services to demonstrate their credentials.

Sites that measure corporate performance

Organisations such as the major superannuation companies and investment professionals often have specialist research teams or consultants dedicated to identifying which companies have a good record on Corporate Social Responsibility. That is how they protect themselves from reputational risk. They have access to search tools such as *Refinitiv, MSCIKLD, Sustainalytics, Bloomberg ESG,* and *RepRisk Ag* to help them evaluate credentials. However, for small businesses there's a limit to how much an individual manager or owner can expect to do on their own to find out about the firms they deal or invest in. If one of your suppliers is using slave labour in another country, how would you know? They don't exactly put it on their label. However, by that very act, they are also implicating you. It's probably not fair of your customers to expect you to have every detail covered, but yet, they sort of do.

Environment – the air, land, and water we share

In this chapter, we will discuss the environment and what it means for businesses. The 'E' in ESG is about the global environment that effectively supports all our businesses; the water you drink, the air you breathe. When we are reporting on ESG we are demonstrating that we are considering the environment in our activities. More than that, we are actually doing something to protect it. There are no standard environmental reports for every type of business. It is up to individual businesses to consider how they will do this. This is about going beyond environmental laws to the small everyday action that values our environment, like reducing plastic waste or changing to renewable energy.

The first problem, economically speaking, is we do not know how to put a value on the environment. We all know it's valuable, but we cannot agree on a 'price.' This makes it hard for modern businesses, because in the past natural resources were considered limitless and there to be exploited; not now. So how do we build in the cost of the ecosystem in the price of the goods we produce? If we compare land for food production versus land for nature, we can provide an economic value for an orchard which is reflected in its real estate value. However, how do you value land that will earn no direct monetary return? More and more natural ecosystems are being relegated to areas that is considered to have little economic land value.

The bigger picture is that natural resources provide ecosystem services to business like clean water, green space, slowing of run-off water, stabilising soils, pollination, and tourism are just some of the benefits offered without charge. If those services are overused, they will be compromised. As a resource, nature needs its own space to regenerate those services.

In some industries we have now reached the limits of a number of natural resources. Perhaps the most visible example is freshwater, certain fish stock, and some wild places. When we say limits, it means they are simply unavailable to most people in some way or they no longer function as they need. Examples include the drought in parts of the United States, overfishing in the Atlantic, and the lack of wild places in Europe. Once these limits have been exceeded beyond a certain point there is not enough money to fix the problem or return them to their previous state.

When we think about the environment from a business perspective, it is worthwhile to consider our individual responsibility. Environmental impact at the beginning of the industrial era was not a strong consideration. Even decades later, few people in the 1950s-60s saw an issue with using fossil fuel or dumping our general garbage at sea. It was the norm at the time – people filled their vehicle at the provided petrol station, and dumped their garbage in the bin, and that was the extent of it. Nobody thought much about where it was finally disposed. Most cities had their untreated sewerage outlets simply piped out to sea. Just in case you thought this was a thing of the past, the sewage treatment plant in Warrnambool Victoria still treats water to a 'secondary' standard rather than a superior 'tertiary' standard, and its existing licence with the environmental watchdog allows the water discharged from the outfall to contain some solids. The water is discharged metres from the shore from an outfall into a rocky reef, and there is even a warning sign to that effect.

As these environmental problems escalated to more global proportions, it was the large corporates that provided the lessons on the risks involved. And, increasingly, their boards and executives counting the cost of poor environmental governance. The world became increasingly shocked at the environmental impact of events like the 'Exxon Valdez', an oil tanker that in 1983 lost 11 million litres of crude oil in a pristine marine environment. Similarly, the 'BP Deepwater Horizon' oil spills in the Gulf of Mexico in 2010, or the tragedy of the 'Bhopal disaster', leaking metho-isocyanate gas killing sixteen thousand people. These are just a small fraction of the environmental and human disasters in the last century. The human and environmental cost is incalculable. As the number of highly visible disastrous issues increased, so did our hesitancy to blindly follow the path forged by the mega corporates. For any organisation, large or small, it begins with one very important step: become aware of your own contribution to the problem. Once you become aware of the risk, you will recognise the steps that you can take to change.

If you as a business are going to make changes, make real changes. If your changes are simply cosmetic then the market will quickly see through this sort of greenwashing, and at that point the trust is irrevocably lost. In this chapter, we will explore some ideas about how businesses might want to think more openly about the environment they share with their customers.

The tragedy of the commons – a cautionary tale

There is a parable often recounted by environmental economists called "the tragedy of the commons" based on an article written by Gareth Hardin in 1968[6]. It's worth reminding ourselves of this moral tale when we think about becoming more environmentally conscious. It cites a story of 1833 on allowing livestock to have open access to graze their stock on the village commons for no payment. This was common practice in that era. If farmer A of the time allowed 2 of his cows to graze on

[6]Hardin, Gareth, 1968. The Tragedy of the Commons: The population problem has no technical solution; it requires a fundamental extension in morality. *Science* 13 Dec 1968 Vol 162, Issue 3859 pp. 1243-1248. American Association for the Advancement of Science.

the commons and farmer B has 4 cows doing the same and neither of them pays, then farmer B benefits twice as much as farmer A. If farmer A then increases his herd allowance to 6 to compensate ... well, you can quickly see where this is going and that self-interest will eventually overgraze the commons and ruin it for all. Hardin refers to the problem of individuals acting in self-interest by claiming if all members in a group used common resources for their own gain and with no regard for others, all resources would eventually be depleted.

The global version of the commons is the air above us, the greater ocean, and the rivers that move water across long distances. Things becomes increasingly tense when there are resources involved such as undersea oil or minerals in places like Antarctica. In fact, it's probably why we put a lot of effort into ownership rights with complicated legal arrangements. In many countries, the land you own as an individual does not extend to the air above you, nor the resources below you. Unfortunately, some of these arrangements fail to be adequate to mitigate a tragedy of the commons, and our atmosphere is one of them.

If we consider the atmosphere and its use as waste sink, but place no value on it, then it is not unexpected that it will be used in an unregulated way. We used to take for granted the role the atmosphere plays in planetary bio-regulation. The waste from burning fossil fuel was always going to increase because there was no cost to the waste component, only the feedstock (coal, oil, and gas).

As a society we simply took all the solar energy trapped as carbon by plants during the carboniferous period which spanned 60 million years and re-introduced it into today's atmosphere by burning it for energy. Great idea at the time - so cheap, but the consequence was releasing way more carbon dioxide into the atmosphere than what currently existed. It changed the earth's climate. It didn't seem like it could be possible in the early days, but it was. Individually we might only do a little bit of atmospheric pollution here and there, but some do a lot more, and, collectively, we do a great deal.

Referring back to Gareth Hardin's article, we can see that our free unregulated 'commons' is now the earth's atmosphere. We use it as a dumping ground for carbon dioxide waste. The gas meanwhile is doing its job of being an atmospheric blanket doubly so. We never saw the implications coming when we dug up oil, coal, and gas, and likely neither did the cow owners on the village commons until things got quite untenable. We should add that we had the scientific warnings about this very early, but governments ignored it for the most part. Scientists first began to worry about climate change toward the end of the 1950s, warning us of the possible consequences[7]. We ignored it early on and we are now living the consequences. At the time many could not believe it was possible and many still deny it today. Funny as it may be, the laws of physics do not really care whether you believe in them or not. Like gravity, they just do their job regardless of your belief.

A reflection of customer attitudes to environment

The average small business has limited ability to influence a market. However, across millions of people, millions of businesses – attitude matters. This can include customers, suppliers, investors, and staff. Therefore, how people perceive the value of an organisation's environmental behaviour can quite quickly become an issue. We say perceived because the facts behind a story can be quite different, but if people judge your organisation to be bad for the environment, things can escalate very quickly and how prepared would you be to respond to critical questions? Do you even have the information at hand to respond?

Results of the Climate Action Survey, carried out by Griffith University's Climate Action Beacon, showed that in 2021 the majority of Australians (72%) believed climate change was cause for concern[8].

---

[7]Revelle, R. and Suess, H, 1957. "Carbon Dioxide Exchange Between Atmosphere and Ocean and the Question of an Increase of Atmospheric CO2, during the Past Decades". *Tellus.* Informa UK Limited. **9** (1): 18–27.

[8]Rosengreen, Carley 2022 "What Australians really think about climate change: survey". Griffith News, Griffith University. April 28, 2022.

This was a shift from 34 percent only a decade ago. This highlights that peoples' attitudes do not exist in a vacuum and there are many who maintain environmental conditions are declining. There are spokespersons of one sort or another in non-profit organisations, academic institutions, and the media to keep the heat on. Many are household name such as Sir David Attenborough, who is probably the world's best-known zoologist. In addition, scientists can now more confidently link local environmental degradation with their causal factors, thereby leaving many organisations exposed if they are contributing to this decline in some way. As a business leader the cost can be very personal.

Changing public attitude is often subtle, but it holds consequences for businesses. There are other more subliminal images that affect our thinking. For example, a climate change protest image of heavily pregnant women carrying banners expressing their concerns about the effect of increasing heat on their foetuses. How do young parents feel when they see this when the news is quoting medical research? How do farmers feel when their community is affected by prolonged drought, ravaged by bushfires, and then suffer flooded crops only months later? Regardless of the potential for recency bias or other contributing factors, our brains are designed to interpret patterns even if all the facts are not yet clear. From an evolutionary perspective, coming to a quick conclusion was an instinctive survival mechanism. This meant nobody waited for scientific confirmation of the possible lion in the bush. When science jumps in with documented probable factors, it will affect people's opinion. When we see images of polluted waterways and mountains of rubbish, does it not impact the people who love walking in nature? It's pretty hard to ignore some of these images. What does that mean for businesses? It means that public attitude will affect how they socially judge your business. It will affect your social license. Take the case of high-end brand Lululemon, a Canadian active wear company known for their strong support for the environment. The company motto is "Be Human, Be Well, and Be Planet", a tilt to the harmonious ideal in line with the yoga world where the brand got its start.

Stating it was deeply connected to the planet, on its sustainability website. They made a virtue of it, but then they were called out for manufacturing in underdeveloped countries using coal-based power which seemed at odds with their messaging. The revelation of its reliance on coal-powered factories in Asia was deemed by its customers as greenwashing, with yoga teachers and students across twenty-eight countries signing an open letter asking Lululemon to source its products from factories using renewable energy. Their manufacturing strategies may not differ to many other companies except their branding around the environment and having a customer base that is strongly interested in environmental issues. If you make strong statements about the environment to attract customers, you need to be able to support those claims. In the end, you have to walk the talk.

One of the more important ethical dilemmas we face is understanding who is responsible for the waste after consuming the product. Is it the manufacturer, the shop, or the consumer? There is no community consensus on this, so it seems the responsibility falls on all of us to some extent. For manufacturers, the choice of packaging is still problematic since it is their much-cherished logo on those packaging, such as fast-food packaging and soda cans that are the ones washing up on previously pristine beaches. Not the photo opportunity they had in mind. Similarly with emissions we are all a bit responsible, it's just that gasses like carbon dioxide or methane are not visible like dead animals entangled in plastic bags. However, the people who make the machines do know how much gas is emitted when the product is used.

If we summarise the current situation, there is a constant stream of messaging about the environmental risk we are facing, and there is a swag of technologies that can point the finger directly at the cause. And it's not always the big corporates anymore.

Now, imagine a person who is deeply concerned about the environment and that person learns that Company X is creating obvious environmental damage in the production of its product. How do you believe this person would react if there was no other product option? If there was another product option? If they were an investor in that company? If they dealt with that company as part of their work? If they worked for that company? Imagine a thousand such people or globally a million such people. What would happen to all that effort in developing brand value? These are the issues that keep corporate CEOs anxiously looking at the future and what their competitors are doing. Like a game of musical chairs, you do not want to be the last to make a move. It's pretty clear when you see that some coal mining licenses that were previously worth billions have now voluntarily been retired by their owners. Coal fired power stations are facing their own existential crisis knowing the clock is ticking. Whether large or small, businesses need to start thinking about how they are perceived relative to their competitors.

Climate change and climate change economics

Let us count the cost. What economists have known for a long time and the public are gradually coming to understand, is there is a cost to taking action and there is also a cost for not taking action. This is not new to businesses but, as is often the case, some decide on action far too late. They may well miss the wave and be left behind. A push by Britain to toughen up corporate environmental disclosures will cast a spotlight on climate change dawdlers as campaigners increasingly turn to the courts to force a speedier transition to a low-carbon economy[9]. Climate change-related lawsuits are on the increase around the world, the bulk in the last seven years according to the London-based Grantham Research Institute on Climate Change

---

[9]Kirstin Ridley and Simon Jessop. 2022. *As Climate Disclosures Toughen, Corporate Laggards May Be Vulnerable to Lawsuits.* Insurance Journal @ insurancejournal.com.

and the Environment[10]. The Governance Institute of Australia published a document in 2020 called 'Climate Change Risk Disclosure: A practical guide to reporting against ASX Corporate Governance Council's Corporate Governance Principles and Recommendations'. Standards Australia is attempting to support these changes by developing an initiative to help guide organisations on the standards, processes, and policies that are required to achieve their ESG goals with an easy-to-access guidance on how organisations can do this in their business[11].

The increasing sophistication of technologies has clearly demonstrated to corporations that they have to take the time to be aware of where the market is moving. Most large corporates are aware of this and devote significant resources to evaluating market trends. If you are a Small to Medium Enterprise (SME), this is difficult to afford, and you rely primarily of the owner's instincts and watching what others are doing.

It is so easy for business to miss the change. Mostly you are too busy dealing with what's in front of you. No one makes time in an over-crowded schedule to think about the hard-to-imagine future risk. We mostly confront the risk issue when something like our insurers walk away. They have long ago done their homework. It's like people who build their business on a coastal headland facing the sea. It's magic until it falls into the ocean. Coastlines move constantly, we know this, and the knowledge exists to assess the risk, but we mostly don't want to know. It's just such an amazing view, right? And the customers love it. It's just the customers do not own it. Change is inevitable, and the key to survival is to see it ahead of time.

If you don't have extensive resources, how do you manage climate change economics? You need to measure the metrics of your business

[10]Joana Setzer and Catherine Higham. 2022. *Global trends in climate change litigation: 2022 snapshot.* Policy Publication, 30 June 2022. London School of Economics and Political Science @ lse.ac.uk

[11]Roland Terry-Lloyd is the Head of Engagement and Strategic Delivery @ standards.org.au

from the most expensive to least and do a risk analysis. Internal measurements allow you to dig deeper into understanding the risk factors. For most businesses, the three major items are staff, energy, and inputs. In this section we will take an environmental lens and other sections will deal with social issues. A lot of this is not, as they say, 'rocket science.'

Staff are important because they have opinions about climate change, and they get to see what is behind the counter. If they do not like what they see, at best they might simply leave for another job and at worst, they can expose poor practices or even sabotage the business. No amount of attempt at coercion is going to stop this happening. The solution is simple – be ethical and invite their help to pivot being more environmentally responsible. As COVID-19 has clearly demonstrated, business doesn't happen without people.

For most companies, energy is the where the action is. It's expensive, and let's face it, our industrial society is almost totally based on fossil fuel for energy. Energy functions that involve industrial systems, like running vehicles, stoves, heating, lighting and so forth, are measurable and can be accounted for. Difficulties arise with rural-related businesses that use biological function (sun, plants, water, and soil) where emissions are not easily measured directly and have to be estimated using calculators. This means relying on someone else's tools to determine your emission factor. An example is agriculture. Growing food crops, orchards, or raising livestock has several calculators that estimate emissions based on the information you put in. Some of these are based on global estimates and may not be accurate for your situation. The result is that many of these calculating tools come up with different answers. So, which one do you choose? Currently, there is no agreed response to this, but the purchasers of the goods are working on what calculators they will accept. In short, know your energy demand and how you might change it – not if, but when you need to.

The last major part of the equation is inputs of goods and services that support your business. You have no direct control over them, so you need to inform yourself of their emission profile much the same as others are doing to you. In some cases, you may have little choice and you simply have to account for it in in your business. This can be time-demanding, but you must consider that your competitiveness in the market will increasingly rely on your knowledge in this area. Large corporations are already doing this. Take for example the port of Newcastle where the main export is coal. They don't mine it, but they recognise they are part of the supply chain. Reading the tea leaves, they have embarked on a program of going with renewables for all their energy needs[12]. This might seem odd for a coal exporter, but they also realise that what they handle as a commodity now, may not support them in the future and they will need to pivot. Taking steps to acknowledge this now, while they have the cash, is a calculated strategy. Future markets can be hard to predict; commodity demands can drop off very quickly and leave you with a stranded asset. Many fossil fuel mining licenses have lost a lot of value over the last decade and in many cases have been surrendered. A great dilemma for the oil and gas sector is that prices are currently at record highs, along with profits. The trick is knowing at what point you should make an exit.

Another example is a chemical company we interviewed who surveyed their customers and decided to look into reports complaining about packaging waste. In consultation with customers, they worked on changing the formulation of their product, increasing its concentration by a factor of ten. This resulted in a huge saving in toll manufacturing, transport, plastic packaging, and storage; and by reducing costs it also delivered an increase in profit by unit of active ingredient. Smart companies are already working with their customers directly to consider what impact their product packaging is having on their customer's waste stream. It's just a small part of building a trusted relationship.

---

[12]Port of Newcastle, 2022. *Port Of Newcastle kicks off the New Year now powered by 100% renewable energy.* News, Sustainability. 05 January 2022 @ portofnewcastle.com.au.

In summary, sooner or later we are going to have to grapple with the issue of economic sustainability. How does what we are putting in our product or services affect society downstream? And how much do we need to question our suppliers about the environmental impact of what they give us? You can pretty much guarantee someone is going to ask you about your environmental impact of your business and not knowing could have a great cost.

Fresh water demand and pollution

According to NASA's Earth Data site, 97 percent of the earth's water is saltwater, leaving a mere 3% as freshwater. Much of this freshwater is locked away as ice or ground water, leaving less than 1% readily available for our use. Clean, fresh water for land animals (including people) is actually quite rare. Just think about this – if the world's water supply were only 100 litres, our supply of fresh potable water would be only about half of a teaspoon. A reflection of our lack of appreciation for this fact, especially in western society, is that we use it to flush our toilets and as a place to dump our waste. This was a cultural norm from a time when water was not regarded as a scarce and expensive commodity.

Producing safe potable fresh water and managing wastewater involves a lot of infrastructure. Local councils are a good source of information about local supplies as they are acutely aware of the situation because they're the ones who must manage it. The importance of fresh water was particularly evident during the years of drought in Australia, when dams dried up and bottled water needed to be trucked into a number of small townships. The more salient irony is that fresh water is most critical on small islands surrounded by water. Salt water.

The question for any organisation is, what is your relationship with fresh water? What is the quality and amount of water you need to operate and how is your waste managed to reduce polluting such a scarce resource? The people living downstream from you are very dependent on how you protect the water that drains to them. Any dirty water you produce doesn't just disappear when out of sight; it goes somewhere and affects someone, including local wildlife. Clearly the market price for water is not reflective of its true value. Its notable that according to the New Zealand Ministry for the Environment that '82 percent of New Zealanders feel that it is very or extremely important to improve the quality of our water'[13].

On the demand side, some industries such as agriculture are highly dependent on large amounts of relatively clean water. The dilemma for such industries is that this is not reflected in the price of their goods. Even where the demand for water goes to the highest value use, market failure is apparent when competitors use poor regulation in other countries to outcompete you. How we manage the sustainability of fresh water with increasing demand is not immediately apparent. We have a great deal of technology we can deploy to measure and track water quality but there is much work to be done around the economics of water. Given that rivers often cross political boundaries, you can expect increasing geo-political tensions over water access.

It all drains to the sea

Not all pollutants are in solution in the water. Some things like plastic bottles, bags, and straws seem to somehow miss the bins and end up in the ocean. A long line of these products, with facemasks being added to the mix more recently with the COVID-19 pandemic, end up in our marine environments, washing up on beaches and shores.

The marine environment is hugely important to us. Not just as a source of food but for its own intrinsic biodiversity value. No one would appreciate having their toilet waste dumped on their front lawn or in their vegetable patch. But for much of the last centuries, that is exactly what we did to our marine environment - the ocean was used as a dumping ground for just about anything, including raw sewage and

---

[13]Ministry for the Environment, 2022. *Understanding New Zealanders' attitudes to the environment.* Research data released September 2022@ environment.govt.nz.

nuclear waste. Even to this day, large cities like Sydney and Melbourne will advise not to swim in wild waterways directly after heavy rains due to potential pollutants making its way to the sea.

Water is known as the universal solvent and, as such, can carry a lot of different materials. Interestingly, chemical laboratories can measure extremely small levels of synthetic products of various types in even large water environments, to the levels of parts per million. Water pollutants can be classified as organic pollutants, inorganic pollutants, pathogens, suspended solids, nutrients and agriculture pollutants, thermal (heat kills wildlife), radioactive, and other pollutants. Organic and inorganic pollutants are mainly discharged from industrial effluents and sewage into the water bodies, which make their way to the ocean. The other items that can move with water are weeds, pest and diseases. Most invasive water weeds came from nurseries, discarded as unwanted plant material. A lot of it can be a non-point source, such as fertiliser, which means we don't exactly know where it came from or how it got into the waterway. But then again, if a business uses specific chemicals and sampling upstream is clear but downstream is not, this pretty much points the finger at that business. It's getting harder for industries to rely on the 'non-point source' pollution maxim; it's really not that hard to find the source of any pollution anymore.

Given the easy visibility of pollutants, what does it mean for businesses? It means that we need to treat water with respect as a limited resource, and we need to look at how we deal with liquid waste and count the cost of proper disposal versus an escalating problem later. This is what we mean when we talk about environmental governance helping to deal with things before, not after, they become a problem that can't be addressed.

Land for nature and agriculture

Human activity takes up land space, whether you need one hectare or thousands of hectares. This requires us to alter the natural environment that was there before. This can be anything from clearing vegetation, to putting in a concrete pad, to bulldozing a road and access through natural bush.

The United Nations Food Agriculture Organisation and the World Bank keep track of population to land area data, and in 1961 there was 23.6 people per square kilometre globally. In 2020, this has nearly trebled to 59.7, begging the question – how does this continue? It's also not evenly spread, with countries like Australia having 3 people per square kilometre, compared to Bangladesh with 1,265. As the population grows, every hectare of land cleared for development means one hectare less the environment has to maintain wildlife. The less land available, the less habitat for certain species, which increases their potential loss, and some species have very specific needs. The ecological details around this topic are huge, but the question most people have is 'what can I do?'

While the internet offers no shortage of ideas about how to be more environmentally friendly, it comes down to the business owner to determine what is realistic in their circumstances. We believe the most important thing you can do is observe what is going on around you and acknowledge that any ongoing loss of habitat is important. Once you have this awareness, you can look more closely at your part in not contributing to this loss more than necessary. In fact, anything you can do to restore wild habitat will be greatly appreciated by the animals and plants that live there. Loss of habitat is a global problem and varies enormously depending on where you are. Land clearing of any form should be the exception not an open license. Land ownership comes with responsibility as its custodian. If we need to clear native vegetation to feed people, fair enough, but we need to consider where that ends. We know that there is price to pay at some point for over-clearing, so how much is too much? This may not please everyone but, at some point, we have to deal with our space problem; there is no planet B and it cannot always be left to someone else to deal with it. This is absolutely a debt on the next generation.

If your operation is going to create significant areas of clearing, you will most likely be asked to provide an impact report before you start. This may be costly and annoying to you but accepting it with good grace demonstrate your sense of responsibility to your customers.

In September 2022, the European Parliament passed a bill requiring EU members to verify whether certain imported agricultural products had been produced in areas linked to deforestation. The regulations also include beef, pork, lamb, goat, and poultry meat, with import of goods produced in areas deforested after January 2020 to be banned.

Land clearing is increasingly moving to a 'make-good' provision due to wildlife habitat loss that has occurred in the past. If you want to clear land today, you may have to consider offsetting the loss somewhere else. To determine what you are having to replace in terms of environmental value requires measured transects across the area concerned to record existing species and inform how important these species are. There needs to be a plan to consider the loss potential. Either way, large levels of clearing may require what is known as 'Environmental Offsets'. These 'offsets' refer to a measure of the downside loss against what you can offer as a protected area to make up for the loss to the same value.

Agriculture is a conundrum for the environment. It takes up large areas to feed an ever-increasing population. At present, agriculture takes up about 37% of the earth's land area, which is quite a lot. Logistically, we are well past the point where everyone can grow their own food. The inefficiencies that go with that would demand more than 50% of our land area. We need innovation as soon as possible, or less people. By innovation we should also consider innovation in business sense. We can, for example, achieve greater efficiency over an area of land where multiple production systems overlap. For example, we have seen hydroponics waste and fish production overlap, vertical gardens and the grazing of orchards and areas under solar panels. These types of multiple land use are highly productive and demand less from unproductive areas.

TABLE 1: Here are some details around current land use from 'Our World in Data'[14].

Earth's surface	29% Land (149 million km^2)	71% Ocean (361 million km^2)
Land surface	71% Habitable	19% Barren + 10% Glaciers
Habitable land	50% Agriculture	37% Forests + 13% others (bush/urban/freshwater)
Agricultural land	77% Pasture livestock	23% Crops

We have already started innovating our food production systems, but it is difficult to tell if this is happening at the rate in which we need to feed the world without destroying much of the natural habitat. It's encouraging that although we saw a steep rise in agricultural land area from 35% in the 60s, to over 40% in the 90s, it has since declined to stabilise at around 37% for the last 25 years. This stability is important, telling us that we are growing more food on the same land area. Given that many agricultural land areas are in a productivity decline, so other areas must be making up the differences.

Food production is non-negotiable. So, agriculture does really have to be sustainable, not just in the word sense "sustainable" but the actual lived reality. Its environmental impact is significant and always will be. It can however, moderate the level of local externalities, and, if highly efficient, reduce pressure on other land areas.

---

[14]Hannah Ritchie and Max Rose. 2019. Website ourworldindata.org accessed in 2019.

Recycling

Recycling seems like a simple idea, but it ends up being quite complex logistically. Let's take plastic for example. Who would have dreamed there were so many different types of plastic and that when it is recycled, they cannot be mixed? Unlike a consumer, as a business it's not likely you are going to work across a large range of different plastics. The main concern businesses need to consider is how to avoid single-use plastics. Whilst packaging is important to manufacturers to protect their new product, it's best not to overdo it or simply have it for show. A lot of overdone packaging is just laziness. As part of the supply chain, it's going to become increasingly important for manufacturers and retailers to take part in the product's life cycle from the 'cradle to the grave.' People are already moving on this, and more product designers are thinking about innovative ideas to support product and package recycling, including biodegradable plastics. Consider coffee takeaway cups for example – once the scourge of cities, they are now becoming less popular after a company found a great replacement to them by introducing regular customers to 'keep-cups.' That is until the COVID-19 pandemic. Now they have another solution, with takeaway coffee cups that are actually recyclable.

The reason for using plastic as an example is that it is highly visible; it's literally everywhere and everyone uses it in some way. If you have customers who are showing signs of concern around packaging waste, you might take note and consider how waste can be repurposed. People are quite inventive and if this is a pain point for your customer, why not be the one who can solve this with ideas? Of greater value is if the repurposing can support a charitable cause.

There are also less obvious waste streams like electronic goods and solar panels that are mixes of product streams. These products are complex and do not fit a single waste stream and would have to be decomposed into multiple waste flows. This is very much the province of engineers but it's worth taking the time to walk around your business and have a look at what ends up in the bin going to landfill. The cost of waste disposal is increasingly going up, and that cost must be borne somewhere in the supply chain. It is also going to be hard to avoid transparency as time goes on, so perhaps it's best to face up to the issue now rather than be unprepared later. In the end it is going to happen. The good news is that, increasingly, people are founding new businesses that are repurposing waste.

A quick take on risk

If you have ever done a risk assessment plan, you would have learned about a 'potential hazard' vs 'the likelihood of the event'. Being on your roof is a potential hazard, the event of you likely falling off will depend on the circumstances at the time and what precautions you have in place. There's a couple of things to note from most major disasters, that occur regularly despite the precautions that have been put in place. The three major causes of most disasters are the original engineering design was flawed, human error (or disregard of the risk), and lack of maintenance around fail-safe mechanisms. Each one is intended to bolster the other but, even in the most diligent operations, the risk of all three failing is real.

You might think of the probability of multiple failures as being extremely unlikely, and this is true. But in real life that's not how it happens. It starts off like that but, over time, failsafe mechanisms do not get maintained properly or they are removed because they are causing delays, such as with the Santiago de Compostela derailment in 2013 when the auto-signalling system was removed to allow the train on older lines. When failsafe mechanisms are no longer working, either actively turned off or improperly maintained, then your probability of a disaster is now much higher.

The reality is we cannot avoid accidents; it's what you do to prepare for them and how you respond that is critical. We have all heard about the need to listen to the experts and it needs to apply here. The need for maintenance, risk analysis, and preparedness is a common mantra of engineers and, yes, it's a big cost. You cannot avoid having to spend money around safety and maintenance, so give it serious consideration.

If you ever have to stand up in front of a news camera or in a court room you will be glad that you actually did take it seriously, not the public relations version of it. I have always wondered about the part where someone starts off a question with, "you should have known or anticipated ..." This is totally a subjective statement but it's a powerful one and lawyers know this. You cannot answer 'yes' and you cannot say 'no' without back up.

Environmental reporting

Let's talk about reporting and the kind of questions you might get asked. What's your energy footprint? What's your waste policy? How do you account for the environmental credentials of you suppliers? What's your product's end-of-life plan? Is anyone going to ask you these questions? Probably not ... so you might think why bother.

Well, they're not the questions the end user customers ask. In fact, they rarely, if ever, ask those types of question of you unless they are another business in your supply chain and they in turn are under pressure from someone else. Across the broader business world, if you do not have any competitors and your product is essential, no problems, your choice. But, if you do have competitors and if any company you supply has committed to be carbon neutral by 2050, or 2030, wherever you are in the supply chain, you can be sure they are going to ask exactly these types of questions. Think of major national events that have publicly indicated the event will be carbon neutral and will be looking for local service and goods suppliers. For them to meet their stated commitment they need for you as a supplier to be doing your part, otherwise how can they possibly meet their goals?

Coles for example have state in 2022 that their ambition is to become Australia's most sustainable supermarket[15]. As one of Australia's leading companies they want to show the way forward as, "by acting together now, we can create a better Australia for future generations. As part of this ambition, we launched our Sustainability Strategy under focus areas *Together to Zero* and *Better Together*". When they say 'together', who are they referring to? They mean this based on their website; "Better Together recognises that when we work together, we can make a real difference to our team, our suppliers, our customers and to the communities in which we live and work". If you are supplier to Coles or a supplier to a company that in turn supplies to Coles you will be asked question about your sustainability credentials. It goes without saying that other retailers will do the same.

The impact of competitors is a risk most businesses understand. When business think of competitors, they usually think of businesses like them supplying the same market. However, competition can also come from new ideas that make what you are supplying redundant. If the new idea is more environmentally friendly than what you offer, this only gives them a greater marketing advantage and most likely hasten your demise. Sometimes the bus that hits you is the one you don't see coming! You need to know where you stand environmentally in relation to the broader business ecosystems.

The process of environmental reporting under ESG is a formal way for you to take stock of your environmental impact. It will encourage you to dig deeper into your business processes to understand their environmental impact. Much the same as you now do for your finances. It is worth noting that a lot of your environmental impact has a cost and will be reflected in your financial accounts such as your energy and waste cost – certainly a good place to start.

---

[15]Coles Group, 2022 Sustainability statement @ colesgroup.com.au.

Strategies for analysing your environmental profile and why you need to

This doesn't need to be a nightmare, but it's also not easy. Using your accounts and a bit of maths, you can do quite a lot of this yourself. It may not be a perfect account of all your business, but it won't be too far out. Remember that at this point small business is not being asked to account for the GHG, but it may in the future. The way to think about it is that all your inputs are costed - fuel, electricity, gas, etc. You can measure what you use to operate the business (except electricity) – this is Scope 1 emissions (see table 2). The next step is to measure the electricity use of your business – this is Scope 2 emissions. Finally, and this is the most complicated you need to identify the carbon footprint of your purchases of good and services that support your business operation across the supply chain. If you don't know what it is, ask the people you have purchased the equipment from, although in many cases they may not know. In that case you are responsible to account for them as part of your footprint. In carbon accounting this is known as Scope 3 emissions - these are the emissions that are created to make the goods you have purchased to run your business. If it's a complex piece of equipment then that becomes very involved, as you keep going up the supply chain. For many businesses about 75% of your emissions come from businesses you deal with that you do not control.

Measuring Scope 3 emissions can be a difficult for small businesses as they usually lack the budgets and internal expertise that larger corporates have for doing carbon accounting. However small businesses can benefit from doing this if they put their mind to it. The value of putting numbers to their emissions and setting a baseline from which to measure progress, will no doubt provide opportunities for managing future risks. This may show new ways to increase efficiency, save money, and become more competitive in the marketplace.

If you want to do a carbon account of your business, you will either need to access help to do the GHG inventory accounting or take the time to learn how you can do your own. You will need to access and become familiar with the Australian National Life Cycle Inventory Database (AusLCI) which is an initiative currently being delivered by the Australian Life Cycle Assessment Society (ALCAS)[16]. Their aim is to provide and maintain a national, publicly accessible database with transparent environmental information on a wide range of Australian products and services over their entire life cycle. It is a tool used by professionals who do environmental assessment and particularly life cycle assessment (LCA), along with protocols for LCA processes for different sectors. You can join for a fee to access the data sets.

Different industry sectors may also have their own specialised calculators that are a good start to approximating your environmental footprint. Here is a table of some of the things you need to consider.

TABLE 2: Explanatory of emission scope.

Scope 1 – This is the direct emission which is generated by the organisation you own or control	This is the energy used in running your vehicle, forklift, or gases from waste compost.	For example, measure fuel and gas use in equipment
Scope 2 – This is the indirect emission you purchase from utilities (Electricity)	This is the electricity or energy used for running plant and equipment	Measure electricity
Scope 3 – This is the indirect emission that is embedded in your upstream and downstream supply chain.	Upstream – This is the embedded energy in the product you have purchased to provide goods and services	Examples include equipment, transportation, travel, and feedstock
	Downstream – This is the emission that is generated by the customer using your product	Examples include use of sold products, end waste

---

[16]The Australian Life Cycle Society ALCAS. https://www.alcas.asn.au/

Currently, one of the more intractable problems is how to manage 'end-of-life.' Not yours, your product's. There is an increasing expectation that if you make a commercial product, you are responsible for that product well after its use is completed and into the last days of its life. The push for regulating this is simple - the cost of managing waste is rising at alarming rates. A good example of this dilemma is managing what is known as "fast fashion" and the mountains of waste it produces. If manufacturers are made responsible for their product to the end of its life, they will be encouraged to design products that will end well. The use of bio-degradable material or recyclable products designed to fit the right waste stream are good examples of changes that companies have adopted. This requires environmental governance to start at the design phase, and it continues, even after you have used it or tossed it into the bin. We are part of a network of consumer goods, and being aware of the decisions we make along the way is the first and perhaps the most important step.

The Australian Packaging Covenant Organisation (APCO) indicated that Australia recycles just 18% of plastic packaging and is well behind to meet its national target of 70% by 2025. They suggest that the current industry-led approach is failing, and stronger laws are needed. The current government is considering this with imposing mandatory packaging rules for industry with design standards and targets – including for recycled content and to address the use of harmful chemicals in food packaging (Environment Minister press release June 9, 2023).

Certainly, minimising the accumulation of useless waste is great start for change, given this is where the industry is moving to. Not creating waste for someone else is another great step. Purchasing only the goods you need and minimising the level of unnecessary cosmetic display will all help. The process of change takes time and money, so getting in early helps get the business better prepared for when the changes are mandated.

A note about reducing emissions versus offsets in the race for carbon neutrality

The key method to mitigating climate change was emission reduction, principally from burning fossil fuel. The use of 'offsets' was meant as a temporary option for economically important functions that had no viable technology to reduce their emissions. It was never intended as an either/or option. Offsets are simply not effective enough to allow the 'business as usual' use of fossil fuel. In any case, there simply is not going to be enough offset available to meet all business demand. It's not hard to see that governments will begin to require those capable of reducing emissions to do so of their own accord and not rely on offsets.

The big picture

The father of ecological economics, Herman Daly[17], was adamant about the relevance of the laws of thermodynamics to economics. After leaving the World Bank in 1994, he outlined how the laws of thermodynamics reveal major flaws within the standard Neoclassical Economic theory. This was very challenging for many. Daly has consistently exposed how such policies have destructive consequences, both socially and environmentally. He advocated that economic growth in the twentieth century had to have boundaries within the natural world. Resources of the planet used in industry are limited and you cannot simply make more. Adam Smith's theory of economic development[18] was developed at a time when the global economy was very much smaller than the natural

---

[17]Herman Edward Daly was an American ecological economist and professor at the School of Public Policy of University of Maryland. He was best known for his time as a senior economist at the World Bank from 1988 to 1994 and for a number of books including *Steady State Theory* (Ed.) an anthology (1973), *For the Common Good: Redirecting the Economy toward Community, the Environment, and a Sustainable Future* (1989), and *Beyond Growth: The Economics of Sustainable Development* (1996).

[18]Adam Smith was a Scottish economist and philosopher who was a pioneer in the thinking of political economy seen by some as "The Father of Economics" or "The Father of Capitalism"; he wrote two classic works, *The Theory of Moral Sentiments* (1759) and *An Inquiry into the Nature and Causes of the Wealth of Nations* (1776).

world, so natural resources were not a constraint to growth. Two and a half centuries later, the global economy is considerably larger and vying for size with the natural world for resources. Daly noted in his speech that the bank should stop counting the consumption of natural capital as income, tax labour and income less, and tax resource throughput more, and we should maximise the productivity of natural capital in the short run and invest in increasing its supply in the long run.

This is not just ideology but integrating economic theory within the laws of physics by acknowledging the limits of certain resources we depend on.

In conclusion, the principle of ESG as it applies to the environment is relatively simple in concept, even if it is not easy to implement. The environment is our shared space. We are all, and we include the natural world as well, tenants in common. There is no other liveable planet within reach if we stuff this one up.

Your business is a legal entity in law and has responsibilities provided by the people who manage it. That responsibility extends to all your other tenants. If we have the capability to significantly change the environment, then we need to do this with due diligence for others who have to share our space.

We cannot change the world economy overnight, but we can do the simplest things towards making our business sustainable by focussing on the waste stream we are creating and valuing the resources we are using. Most actions will flow from that.

Social – working within your community

et us once again reiterate, this is a discussion, not a definitive text on corporate social obligations. It's a discussion about how a business might conduct itself within a community. The 'social' in corporate governance refers to all your stakeholders, all the people likely to have a material impact on your business. *Who are your stakeholders?* is a good question for you to consider. It may be far wider than you might realise. You are now part of a global community; this means that people on the other side of the world can materially impact your business. If you have been too busy working in the business to step outside of it for a while, now is the time to have a good look around. This conversation is exactly about stepping out of the business and looking at your role in the broader community. We cannot offer a recipe for what action is required, but we will highlight some of the public relations risks you might face if you get things wrong.

Let us start with a simple principle of human relationship: trust. This underpins all business relationships. Lack of trust adds a cost to any business, and it is why we put so much emphasis on contracts. It takes time and a keen awareness of stakeholders to build real trust. This is important because we can become complacent about the way we see our business; we know it so well we can become blind to the changes, good and bad. The reality you face about how the business might be under-performing might be uncomfortable, but it is fundamental to risk management. You simply cannot control everything around your business. This leads on to the second part and it's about building real value that meets external expectation, sometimes referred to as goodwill. You cannot climb out of a public relations disaster without having built a degree of social capital in the first place.

What do we mean by social capital? This is the value we get from positive connections between people. In business this is described as a set of various good working relationships you have, reputations you have achieved, and the people or brand assets existing within an organisation. If you have good social capital, you can be forgiven some mistakes.

How we consider reality and build social capital is the focus of this chapter. We will deal with rights more broadly and look in a little more detail at some of the things that are top of mind in the media.

Diving into the rights of the community

Let us go straight into the issue of 'rights' mentioned in the introduction. Businesses must consider the rights of their broader stakeholders. This includes staff, customers, suppliers, the general community, and of course the environment. This is particularly important for those members of the community who are disadvantaged and may not have the resources to assert their rights (e.g., minors and vulnerable people). The environment also cannot directly assert its rights, but it is represented by government agencies and organisations who will act on its behalf. If you understand and respect these rights, it is no longer an adversarial situation. To put it simply, there needs to be mutual respect between you and the other party.

An imbalance of power in asserting your rights is something for businesses to take great care in managing. Just because a community group do not (or does not know how to) assert their rights does not mean they are not entitled to those rights. The process in which negotiations are undertaken should be justifiable as being equitable. Courts may well find in favour of those who did not have the option to draft the contract of agreement. If you set unfair terms and conditions, you may find yourself liable for rectification.

Clashes over land use and cultural heritage are clear examples of complicated rights issues that hold different levels of power. Whether it's mining, agriculture, development, nature reserves, or Indigenous land rights, they all have their rights to exist and not be impinged upon. How to reconcile these multiple rights is not easy and, while money may assist some areas, the community will also have their say in the court of public opinion. You need only look at the fallout for Rio Tinto, which faced some heated public and political backlash after deciding to blow up 46,000-year-old Aboriginal rock shelters at Juukan Gorge in Western Australia, to expand their mining operation. Given this went against the rights of the land's Traditional Owners, it prompted a federal inquiry and led to the resignation of their former chief executive Jean-Sebastien Jacques. The legacy of that is ongoing not only for the company but also for other resource companies.

As an entity, you have certain rights, but if in asserting your rights you impinge on someone else's rights, you might expect a level of pushback. Where that can end is hard to predict. There is also an emerging argument about the rights of global citizens in the face of climate change and the industries that are responsible for most of the emissions. Expect this to become increasingly important. The images of people affected by natural disasters is continuous across the globe and those affected are demanding action. Large polluters will be required to act to manage this type of risk. This may not directly affect small businesses who are not large emitters, but they can become indirectly affected as part of the supply chain. The power of large corporates is that they can shift the risk across their broader supply chain. Large companies will inevitably push back across their Scope 3 emissions and the cascade affect will eventually affect small businesses.

Social license, so what is that?

A license is a ticket to operate. Usually this is issued by a regulator, however a social license is one issued by society. Any persons that your business impacts in some social ways are part of your social responsibility. Your social license is your contribution to society in demonstrating that you are a good corporate citizen and therefore given public license to operate. We do not really have a measure for it, but you will certainly know if you do not have it. You will clearly see customers and perhaps staff begin to walk away.

It comes broadly under the need for business to demonstrate social justice; it's not in any traditional business manual but refers to what is the social expectations at the time, and that can be very broad. It can be such things as community acceptance of a local development project or 'equal pay for equal work' regardless of gender or race. This was certainly not the social expectation 100 years ago, but it is now, even if it still falls short in many places. Today, the expectation is increasingly for businesses to demonstrate social equity and inclusion in their workforce. To have genuine conversations with their community stakeholders. They are also expected to provide goods and services that do not exploit the environment, and to demonstrate a level of environmental responsibility in the process. Many older employers who have lived in a different generation can sometimes forget younger employees were brought up with different cultural expectations.

As the business owner or board member you are expected to provide the lead in your obligations. A business as an 'on paper' entity is not able to do this, it depends on the human judgement of its trustees. There is some conjecture as to whether a board is only responsible to shareholder value, as it used to be thought, or to the broader community. Corporate governance is suggesting the goal post is moving in this area, especially around climate change and social impact. It is difficult, for example, to carve out shareholder benefits as being totally separate from climate change obligation or gender equity. Shareholders are directly asking for action on this front to protect their future asset. This is more evident of long-term shareholders rather than the high turnover 'buy/sell' share market professionals. There is a divergence of opinion between short-term returns and long-term shareholder value, the latter being more concerned about corporate social license. Small businesses are in the main long-term concerns, so social license should be on your radar.

Your moral obligation

Being 'moral'[19] can look a bit different to different people, but the essence of immorality or 'wrongness' can be universal. Many societies consider being deceitful to be wrong. Again, we can see that being deceitful as human beings may gain a degree of evolutionary advantage for a time, but being found out usually resulted in severe punishment when survival was precarious. However, it does often make people angry enough to take some form of decisive action. If a brand you strongly supported was outed as exploiting child labour, your values would prompt you to question whether you will continue to support the brand in question.

There is now a whole branch of research around 'Business Ethics' because consumers are looking for products that fit their values. Increasingly, employees are also looking to work for organisations that align with their values. Organisations are now being judged both internally and externally. While immoral operators certainly exist, they are usually smart enough to realise they must be seen to be moral, as they are mostly outnumbered by moral ones they depend on.

We are all aware trust is very slow to build and can evaporate very quickly. Business will sometimes look for a shortcut and employ a trusted celebrity or influencer to tout their brand. All very well, providing the celebrity in question continues to meet social expectations.

---

[19]Morals in this context refers to a sense of right or wrong. Ethics, on the other hand, refer more to principles of "good" versus "evil" that are generally agreed upon by a community.

At time they do not, there is hasty exit to denounce said 'brand ambassador.' Celebrities command big dollars because they are generally trusted, until they aren't. Poor behaviour by someone endorsing a brand reflects badly not only on the celebrity but can also impact the brand. In a world highly attuned to social media, it doesn't take much when something as simple as a questionable statement on social media from a brand ambassador can very quickly go viral. It is interesting to consider the large sums firms will pay for accessing community trust. There have been some spectacular fails of those brands with celebrity scandals. Lance Armstrong reportedly lost $75 million in sponsorship deals when he was found guilty of doping. Tiger Woods, Michael Phelps, and Michael Vick are all famous athletes who damaged the brands they were associated with, costing them, and the brands they represented, hundreds of thousands of dollars. And then there are the brand ambassadors who don't even use the product they are being paid to promote. Charlize Theron appeared at a press conference for an Austin film festival wearing a Christian Dior watch, having signed a 14-month contract, worth $3 million, with Swiss watchmaker, Raymond Weil. That's how much trust is valued, although we still maintain that your best brand ambassadors are your existing employees, and you already pay them.

The important question for SMEs is: even if it were not so expensive, would you really want to take the risk of trying to buy trust? To hand that responsibility over to an external party you do not actually really know that well? Why is that important? Because trust is pretty much first in business. If that is so, then paying attention to your moral obligation is how you build real long-term trust. It is about the relationship you have with your customers. The customer is not always right, but they should at least be heard.

Who is your community and why is it important?

As most managers will often bemoan, dealing with 'things' is far simpler than people. But it is the people who allow a business to exist. We also tend to treat the business as another person in the community. So much so in fact, that legally we give a business the status of a person. They can perform transactions, own things, pay taxes and, importantly, they are held accountable for what they say and what they do. The CEO and board members act a bit like a parent. No CEO or board member ever wants to get a call from the media asking for a comment on some issue relating to their business. That is rarely good news.

Let us dig into the reality a bit more and consider that your business lives in a particular community. Mostly it is the community of people where your products or services are purchased. Most businesses are aware of this, but it is time consuming to investigate how your business is perceived by a community, and you may be in more than one type of community. We are not referring to a geographical community, but a consumer community. If you sell hiking equipment, you are involved in a particular group of people: hikers. If you make boats, you aren't necessarily selling to hikers. Communities are not homogeneous; they vary in a spectrum of attitude, and it is easy to stick to the one you are most comfortable with. However, your business can be affected by parts of the community that you have nothing to do with. They are secondary or even tertiary influencers to the business. These secondary influencers are the groups of people who are not likely to buy or use your product directly, but can exert an influence on your primary customers and play an important role in their buying decision. Hence why it is important for companies to understand who these influencers are and what messaging you might need to consider in order to support a positive attitude towards your primary customers. Secondary influencers can be anyone such as children, spouses, friends, neighbours, and associates. We often see this from car salespeople who have pivoted to the fact that purchasing a car is not reliant on one gender or age group, or that children can have a big say in family purchases. Similarly holiday destinations are made by considering the whole family, given that nothing will spoil your holiday more than being saddled with bored, grumpy kids.

Think for a moment, for example, who really makes the decision about the mobile you buy for your teenagers? Or the cereal you buy the kids?

External events can exert a strong influence on a community and can play a very important role in your business having to adjust. If there is a widespread shortage of certain goods, the price will go up. If, however, you are seen to be taking advantage of shortages by price gouging, you can lose a lot of that social capital very quickly. How companies behave in the here and now when the community is under pressure is going to be remembered.

Sometimes doing the right thing by the community can have a real cost and there are many such examples where companies have absorbed a cost to support their community and in turn built their social capital. During Covid-19 lockdowns the local café pivoted to supplying people with prepared take-away meals at very good prices. As well, many gyms and other service business offered online options to support their clients. They do this for a very good reason - to protect the broader business over the long term, and it is absolutely something every business needs to consider. If customers feel cheated and lose trust, they can walk away and there is every chance they will find a viable alternative and not come back. Remember, aside from running a business we are also customers, and we see some of this inside ourselves. In the end, your best advisor is inside you when you are on the other side of the counter. Treat your customers as you would expect to be treated.

So how do you build social capital? It can happen quickly and organically through the steady and diligent widening of your community horizon; set aside time to be aware about what is happening in your community, and beyond. Active listening is an important tool to learn about what is going on around you. All communities have influential leaders; take the time to have a genuine conversation with them and get them to help you understand what they know. They are community leaders for a reason. This makes you more prepared to deal with the unexpected, even if it is not what you thought it was going to be. It's about you being on guard to the need for change. Markets talk about "Black Swan" events as a metaphor that describes rare, unexpected events that have significant impacts on society and global economies. The fact that the only swans ever observed in the northern hemisphere were white does not mean that black ones do not exist, as was the case for Europeans until they came to Western Australia. Without overdoing the metaphor, the underlying importance of black swan events is that something that has never happened before can occur in your future. It is also important for businesses to understand that any enterprise can be deeply affected by community expectations, even if they are a long way from your direct customers. The trick is not to be ready for anything specific, because you do not know what that will be, but to have a "being ready" mindset. Having such a mindset means you prepare, and you get up more quickly when the hit comes.

Customers, the final arbiter

You would like to think you can influence your customer, but in so many ways you do not, despite what advertising companies tell you. Not that advertising does not help, it certainly does, but it is not the only perception people will hold of your business. If a friend says this tyre company, this restaurant, or that show is bad or is good; most people are less likely to fact-check the background details before making a decision on whether to purchase this product or not. Like most of us, you know your friends well enough to know how closely your taste are alike, but the business in concern is an unknown quantity. We are also more prone to believe a negative assessment than apositive one. Ask yourself, have you ever checked customer ratings like Trip Advisor and had second thoughts about buying a product? Our brain does not deal with absolute reality, it uses shortcuts or what are known as heuristics. These shortcuts approximate the image of your business, so how you are perceived depends on what shortcuts people are relying on. That great advertising photos for a holiday destination may not be the same as the old and shabby hotel lobby you walk into. Even if the product is great, we have already anticipated that things are not likely to get better from the first impression, and that anticipation often becomes a self-fulfilling reality. Interestingly, what changes customers attitude is the quality of the people your customers interact with and how honest they are. A genuine smile goes a long way.

Apart from quality, a good reputation helps enormously. Examine your own motives for shopping where you do, and you will most likely find a type of confirmation bias for doing so. This is not a marketing text, so we will not go into those details of image branding, this is about your public image in terms of your customers perception of your community values. This is a hard thing to measure, but if you get a sense of what it is, that is great. Just note, public perception or trust is a fragile thing, and it can shatter in a heartbeat. There is no substitute for being involved in your community, whether it is a local sports club or art activities. People want to deal with people. In that regard can we say frontline staff are absolutely critical! We are going to emphasise this again, absolutely critical. They can make or break your business and we hear this so often and we think it is astounding that they are often the lowest paid, the least trained staff member. How is this possible? This is the first real 'people impression' customers have of your business.

Influencers

We have all heard about influencers on social media, there are however lots of other influencers and they abound in any community. Publican, priest, or the local comedian, what they say influences your outlook. Since most of us have an imperfect view of the businesses around our town, what they say will unconsciously affect your perception. We tend to add bits and pieces of information together and make a judgement. Most of us are simply too busy and preoccupied with other things to do a thorough fact check. This might seem a little unfair, but that is how it works; we are quick to judge and slow to change our initial judgement. How you counteract that is by putting effort and resources into being part of the community. There is no set recipe for this as communities are all a bit different.

Influencers, by the way, are not fact checkers either, and they are just as easily influenced by perception as the rest of us. The difference is they have a megaphone and if they get it wrong well it is, 'oops sorry about that,' and they move on while you pick up the pieces. It may not be fair, and most likely was not intentional, but it is reality. It's ironic that we often put some much energy in trying to convince people they are wrong, when reality would suggest that people rarely listen to what you are saying - how often have people considered what you have said and then admit they were wrong?

This is why community social capital is built as insurance against events you do not have much control over. The social in ESG is more than lip service, it is understanding and preparing for any number of unknown risks that may come your way. It is about accepting that you, as in the business, have social obligations as a member of the community.

Regulators

Regulators, on the other hand, are fact checkers - obsessively so. They love details, especially yours. While your moral obligation in supporting your community is not on their radar, misleading the community definitely is. Obviously, being detailed takes a lot of resources so their capacity to investigate more broadly is limited, but should you come into their sights from poor behaviour, expect a thorough scrutiny.

Whatever claims a business puts up in the public space in terms of advertising, either on their website, media, Facebook page, or instore is fair game for verification. Regulators are not that numerous on the ground, but customers are, and if they detect a degree of falsehood, they will not keep it to themselves. It is certainly the case that people who 'overshare' can be bad for business. There is also nothing to stop regulators from picking up areas to target from social media. A major target of ASIC at present is corporate greenwashing on the basis that customers do make product choice on stated environmental credentials.

Listed companies have annual reports and within their pages you will find some of the claims made by companies. The details around these claims are subject to legal accounting by the regulators and shareholders. However, for unlisted companies there is no such reporting, but they are still at the mercy of public opinion. If you are a small unlisted company competing with a large public listed company, it's in your competitor's interest to hold you accountable to public opinion as a way of levelling the playing field. In corporate competition playing nice is rare. If you are at risk of poor public opinion, then that is a vulnerability of your business. If you have stepped over the line from poor public opinion to misleading customers, you could end up in a whole world of pain aided and abetted by both customers and your competition.

An example was a media release by ASIC that it had taken action for greenwashing against listed energy company Black Mountain Energy Limited (BME)[20]. The company was fined $39,960 in regard to three infringement notices issued in relation to concerns about alleged false or misleading sustainability-related statements made to the Australian Securities Exchange (ASX) between 23 December 2021 and 8 September 2022.

ASIC was concerned that BME either did not have a reasonable basis to make the representations, or that the representations were factually incorrect. Incidentally, payment of an infringement notice is not an admission of guilt or liability, but you do end up with an image problem. So not only do you get fined by regulators, but you are also outed as being misleading in a public statement. The lesson is: be

---

[20]Media Release, Thursday 5 January 2023, 23-001MR ASIC issues infringement notices to energy company for greenwashing. Australian Securities & Investment Commission (ASIC).

mindful of what you published about yourself. Do you have the evidence to back up the claims?

Suppliers (peers)

Suppliers are key stakeholders as part of your supply chain, so you may put a degree of trust in the material they supply you. Should you? Well, you would think that surely, they would be taking a big risk if they knowingly lied about the provenance or quality of their product. But suppliers can mislead you intentionally or unintentionally, and it could hold serious consequences for you. Unfortunately, there are always some businesses in the market that cannot see past the profit. Anything that is found to be a direct lie or being deliberately deceitful will not only put their business at risk, but yours as well. If you are a builder, for example, and you have unknowingly used defective products, how will this work when the issue becomes apparent?

Let us consider an important case highlighting such an issue. After the UK's Grenfell Tower disaster in June 2017, where an apartment fire went so quickly out of control due to flammable external cladding. The safety of cladding came under close scrutiny. Properties all over the world were found to be at high risk and recladding became of urgent necessity. Suddenly, either the homeowners or the builders were faced with massive renovation costs. To highlight the dilemma faced by all parties, Master Builders Victoria wrote to the Victorian State Government to express its concern and call for changes to the Cladding Safety Victoria Bill 2020. They outline that the consequence of the legislation will see builders vulnerable to claims that they can neither have foreseen, nor protected against. The claims would leave many builders insolvent. They may well have used these products in good faith but the cost consequences of having to replace a safety hazard has left no one happy.

Although a lot of building material that hold some degree of risk such as sealant, brackets, or timber may not be that serious, but simply accepting the quality standard of a supplier on paper can be incredibly costly. Many car manufacturers have faced similar issues defending legal actions and at the same time making good with expensive recalls and repairs. A clear example was the 2018 global Takata airbag recall affecting millions of vehicles. In some cases, it was more reputational damage than driver safety risk, as was the case for the Volkswagen in September 2015; the United States Environmental Protection Agency (EPA) issued a notice of violation of the Clean Air Act to German automaker Volkswagen Group. Volkswagen was found to have intentionally programmed their diesel engines to activate their emissions controls only during laboratory testing, although in real world driving conditions the vehicles emitted up to forty times more nitrous oxide levels.

Another key factor in the supplier relationship is pricing. With long supply chains, especially international ones, changes in geopolitical situations can make pricing now and pricing later quite different. This means that cost estimates and reliability for you to deliver can quickly become problematic. Hence the relationship, trust, and communication you have with your supplier is vital.

The big issue for many SMEs is that they simply do not have sufficient resources to background check their suppliers or hold them to account in times of shortage. As a small business, you should be alert however to anything that appears to be competitively too good to be true.

It is a given that big companies have the advantage of deep pockets to weather these storms, but what about SMEs? Ask yourself, could you as a small business find the reserves to survive severe reputational damage? If the answer is no, then managing reputational risk becomes an important consideration.

Occupational health & safety

Obligations for occupational health and safety is covered under various State Work and Safety Acts. Most of these Acts have been around for decades, so we will not cover your legal obligation as a business here. However, there are two things we should note. One is that management should pay particular attention to complacency in their OH&S processes. Too often processes become a tick-a-box exercise and oncoming risks are missed. The big issue that cannot always be covered by a process is 'fatigue,' which is very hard for employers to enforce, so they must rely on supporting a culture of staff taking personal responsibility. It is important for employers to ensure that expectations of work outputs are not counterproductive to the messaging. For example, the law may require delivery drivers to have fatigue management plans, but that message can be lost if bonuses are given for faster or greater volume of deliveries. People will by nature use 'workarounds' to push themselves to achieve the bonuses. The NSW Government established an investigative Taskforce led by SafeWork NSW and Transport NSW to examine whether any avoidable risks may have contributed to a number of recent fatalities of food delivery riders in late 2020. The report indicated that one of the common hazards that needed to be managed included "unrealistic estimated delivery times" resulting in time pressures and unsafe riding[21]. The work around by the employer in this case was, they were "contractors," not "employees."

The second thing we might note is the issue of mental health of workers. This has been an emerging issue for many years but was accentuated with the COVID-19 pandemic. Mental health should not be conflated with mental illness or disorders any more than physical health and a disease condition. Consider very carefully the mental health and fitness of your employees. The main areas of concerns are bullying, sexual harassment, work-related stress, and poor work-life harmony. It is worth taking time to consider how you are addressing this.

---

[21]Swanston, T. Mon 8 Feb 2021. New guidelines to protect food delivery riders after spate of deaths on Sydney roads. ABC News

Your mindset should be on employee safety, not simply meeting the regulatory requirements. It should be part of the culture of the organisation.

Modern slavery and child labour

We won't go over the details of the *Modern Slavery Act* (2018) but suffice to say that those of us who have ever purchased anything at an almost unbelievably cheap price were unwittingly supporting this practice. According to British-based Anti-Slavery International, there are 49.6 million people living in modern slave conditions (forced labour and forced marriage[22]). This is an increase of 10 million since the last global estimates in 2017, and 1 in 4 are children, with fifty-four percent of them being female. "Sweat shops", as they are often referred to, are not very visible in Australia, but they do exist. The University of Sydney estimated that up to 15,000 people are living in conditions of modern slavery in Australia[23]. It is a crime, and the perpetrators mostly prey on the vulnerable who do not have support as citizens, do not know their legal rights, or are intimidated by their operators. The dilemma for a lot of businesses is that suppliers offering cheap goods and services are not transparent about their labour source. Costs are critical when margins are tight, but at what point do you draw the line? It may also transpire that your customers will draw the line for you.

The majority of supported modern slavery occurs via offshore factories in under-developed countries where workers do not receive a living wage. A number of fast-fashion brands were exposed using these types of suppliers in 2015 and again in 2016[24]. It's not only goods suppliers, but waste disposal companies; waste is shipped to

---

[22]Anti-Slavery international is a UK based charity founded in 1839.

[23]University of Sydney's Modern Slavery statement, June 2022.

[24]Gupta, S and Gentry, J. 2018. Evaluating fast fashion: Fast Fashion and Consumer Behaviour. Book chapter in Eco-Friendly and Fair. Researchgate.net/publication/330769666.

countries where environmental regulations are poorly supported or enforced[25].

Organisations are increasingly requesting more information around suppliers' work practices during the contracting stage. Small businesses may not have the influence of large operators, but they still need to consider if what they are being supplied is going to meet customer expectations. Some businesses have made ethical standards a virtue in promoting their businesses, urging customers to vote for a fairer world with their wallet. While price is still mostly king, it is changing for a large part of the community. They are questioning provenance a lot more than they used to, and they are prepared to pay a bit more for the right product.

In turn, companies with turnovers upwards of $100 million, as well as all Australian federal government agencies, are now formally required to report on how they have managed their due diligence in ensuring the have not supported modern slavery. Under the *Modern Slavery Act*, businesses are required to actively avoid modern slavery risks throughout their supply chain. This means the large corporations you may supply will inevitably weigh the risk of dealing with you and impose a requirement for you to report on your efforts in this regard. Once again, it will cascade from large corporates to their smaller suppliers.

Underpaying workers is not just a legal issue but also has a high level of reputational risk attached whether its local or overseas. Generally, the reputational risk has a higher cost than the legal one. Underpayment of workers tends to make good headlines for news outlets. We have noted that a lot of media outlets were quite willing to call out existing brands they alleged underperform in this area in 2022.

---

[25]Funnell, A. 2022. Fast fashion is getting faster with data-driven designs but experts worry about its environmental impacts. ABC News. March 2022.

Sexual harassment and bullying

There are a number of social issues that all businesses should consider, such as various forms of bullying or sexual harassment. This can occur both within the business, but also to customers. What can start as unwanted humour can escalate. Do not ignore persistent rumours, and ensure you provide a safe space for complaints. The risk for businesses is that poor behaviour by those in power result in either valuable people simply leaving the organisation, or legal and reputational damage may follow. Regardless of business risk, there is moral element to this type of behaviour, and you have a duty of care towards your staff and customers. The impact on the victim is lifelong. If you are in charge of an organisation, be very aware of internal behaviour. If it comes to a court situation, you will be asked about your level of awareness; if you were not aware, why not? Being high in management is not a mandate for being right. The value that senior managers bring to the organisation as the financial 'rainmaker' can easily be undone with poor behaviour. Genuine exit interviews are critical to taking the pulse of the organisation. We realise most small businesses do not have a human resources department, so it unfortunately falls to you as the owner or the board to manage this either internally or with the support of contractors. In some way, external contractors provide a more impartial view of internal issues, not being caught up in the day-to-day internal politics of an office.

There have also been cases where harassment was external to the organisation. In one case, a corporation speaking anonymously reported the need to step in when one of their contractor's staff was reportedly thought it was funny to be heckling females passing by on a city construction site. It's important to understand that sexual harassment doesn't need to be physical. Given the company's logo was all over the site, this reflected poorly on them when the complaints started rolling in. The company called in the contractor to stop work until the issue was addressed. This highlights issues can come from anywhere. No one negotiating the contract felt the need to have included specific clauses to that effect, but your pattern of behaviour is not someone else's. This is why having strong behavioural guidelines already in place can quickly allow you to respond.

For senior managers or executives often asked to social networking events involving alcohol, this can be a huge risk area. While being intoxicated is often used as a defence of poor behaviour to mitigate reputation, it doesn't absolve anyone from the responsibility of what they have done. Neither is the defence 'it was just a bit of harmless fun'; your humour is someone else's offence. When you see it in a court transcript it loses the humour element.

Demanding respectful behaviour at all times towards your staff and empowering them to call it out is valuable. It's good for staff morale if they feel you have their back. Listening to staff is an important way of learning what is going on inside your business. As part of your social responsibility, you can start to become aware of what your organisation is thinking and take some steps to demonstrate you are listening.

Discrimination

The Australian Commonwealth, States and Territories have laws that prohibit various types of discrimination. They cover areas such as race, gender, religion, political opinion, national extraction, social origin, age, medical record, criminal record, marital or relationship status, impairment, mental, intellectual, or psychiatric disability, physical disability, sexual orientation, and trade union activity. Though comprehensive, the laws are unfortunately applied in slightly different ways, and there are some gaps between different states and territories, as well as at the Commonwealth level. There are also exceptions, and many things fall through the cracks because it's hard to prove low level discrimination and many workers do not feel they have the capacity or resources to call it out. Yet, sometimes when one person calls it out, there is a domino effect as others feel more empowered to call out discrimination. The question that will be asked is: were you aware of this in the first instance? If not, why you were not aware? Things can look obvious in hindsight, the things you missed when your mind was preoccupied with other matters.

To work out your obligations you will need to check the Commonwealth legislation and the state or territory legislation in each state in which you operate. You will also need to check the exemptions and exceptions in both the Commonwealth and state/territory legislation, as an exemption or exception under one Act will not mean you are exempt under the other. Alternatively, you might consider examining any unconscious bias[26] you may harbour towards discrimination and put some strategies to mitigate it.

Discrimination is insidious, and much of it is an unwillingness on our part to acknowledge this unconscious bias we all have. Every one of us carries a level of unconscious bias where our brain takes a short cut and makes a value judgement of people with little to no evidence to support this view. Our default is we often make a snap judgement of people within the first few seconds of meeting them. It takes a fair bit of effort to suspend judgement and wait for more evidence, but that is exactly what we should do.

The impact of this on the business is we end up with a lack of diversity. We may end up hiring only people like us and miss opportunities. High performing business generally have greater diversity[27]. This only works if managers or boards intentionally and meaningfully do take steps to include it as part of the selection process. If there is no one who feels free to challenge a decision and offer an alternative, there is

---

[26]Unconscious bias is defined prejudice in favour or against a thing, person or group. See article by Dr Cat Adams at the Unconscious Bias project (202). https://www.unconscious-biasproject.org/resources/explain-unconscious-bias.

[27]Dixon-Fyle, S., Dolan, K., Hunt, V. and Prince. 2020. Diversity wins: How inclusion matters. McKinsey report May 2020.

a very real risk the business will miss emerging opportunities or risks. This is also covered under Gender and Diversity in the Governance chapter.

The public challenge to discrimination is becoming louder and increasingly clever in the digital age. To limit bias, Canadian government officials tested a blind hiring initiative designed to reduce unconscious bias and promote gender and ethnic equality. Blind hiring is any technique that anonymizes or "blinds" demographic-related information about a candidate from the recruiter or hiring manager that can lead to bias[28]. The reason for this type of initiative is highlighted by Forbes, who indicated that job applicants from minority groups are "whitening" their resumes by deleting references to their race with the hope of boosting their shot at jobs, and recent research shows the strategy is paying off for them[29]. This highlights a level of existing unconscious bias in the selection process. Their research indicated that white-sounding names on resumes are 75% more likely to get an interview request than identical resumes with Asian names and resumes with male names are 40% more likely to get an interview request than similar resumes with female names. Generally, there is no legal recourse following from these actions as they are hard to prove individually, but there could be reputational damage if there is a detected consistent pattern. Many businesses rely on the aggrieved party's inability to clearly demonstrate a substantial bias. This is very difficult to prove, but the legislation is there.

Animal exploitation

This is another social area gaining traction. Animals have no means of speaking up for their rights as humans might; they cannot challenge

[28]Min, Ji-A. 2017. Blind Hiring: A How-To Guide To Reduce Bias & Increase Diversity. Ideal. com recruiting blog June 8 2017.

[29]Gerdeman, D. 2017. Minorities Who 'Whiten' Resumes Get More Job Interviews. *Harvard Business School Working Knowledge* looks at the latest research and ideas from the faculty of Harvard Business School.

poor practice. So, the laws on what constitute good animal welfare practice is reliant to some extent on public response about what is acceptable or not. Although many who raise domestic animals are very respectful of the welfare of their charge, they are often frustrated by other poor actors in their industry. There is a diverging public opinion about the use of domestic or farmed animals as a source of protein or for sport, but consumers have the choice. Your stakeholders are also people who will often be presented with news being sourced from various activist and organisations that monitor the care of animals. If your name comes up in relation to a poor practice, then that can quickly become a problem. This has been major issues for the proponents of the live export trade, the racing industry, laboratory testing of animals, whaling, circuses, zoos, hunting events, and the fur trade. Emerging places of contention are puppy farms, intensive livestock farms and fisheries, wet markets, and the practice of wild animal culling. Basically, there is a long list and even if you do not directly deal with animals, there is every likelihood you are a supplier or a customer of a business dealing with animals.

In terms of ESG, there is a measure by some investors of what percentage of their portfolio might be exposed to companies flagged for involvement in animal welfare, or "Fund Animal Welfare Involvement". A lower score means lower exposure to companies involved in likely animal welfare issues. Typically, investor information organisation such as 'World Animal Protection'[30] allocates superfund investors by categories including involvement in live animal export, cosmetic testing, and intensive production amongst a number of categories.

ESG defines animal welfare as companies involved in testing products or product ingredients of any sort on animals, breeding animals for animal testing purposes, exhibiting animals, and operating factory farms. This includes publicly traded companies that perform

---

[30]https://www.worldanimalprotection.org.au/take-action/super-funds

testing activities in-house, as well as those outsourcing testing to third parties.

ESG doesn't mandate any views on what you should or shouldn't be doing, but it is about reporting honestly what your involvement consists of. It recognises that investors or the buying public have a right to know your level of involvement in managing animal welfare. The rights of animals are more formally covered by the legal requirement in whatever jurisdiction you operate.

For companies directly involved in poor practices there is nowhere to run from exposure in this area, especially in an era where everyone carries a camera. While some of it is misunderstood intentions, poor animal practices are simply poison to businesses regardless of circumstances. While laws around animal exploitation fall short of human exploitation, the public response of outrage is just as high.

Social reporting

For unlisted companies there is no requirement for any ESG social reporting unless you have a board that specifically wants this as part of their board discussion. However, given some of the risks that may emerge from, say, poor public messaging, it would certainly pay for a board or a business owner to ask the more pertinent questions. You are expected to be on top of your financial reporting but what about the other risks? The questions you might ask yourself are:

- How well do I understand what is going on with our staff? Are there issues that are likely to become a problem for the business that I am not seeing?
- How do our customers perceive us beyond the obligatory surveys? Do we have an in-depth understanding of how the business is travelling, are we seen as a company of the future? Can we answer their questions openly and honestly?

- What do we really understand about the risks in our supply chain? Does this need re-examination? What am I likely to be asked as a supplier? Do we ask enough questions of our own suppliers, or do we just accept what they tell us?
- How are we perceived by the general community where we do business? Are we in touch with community trends and expectations? Are there opportunities we are missing? Are there risks we are not seeing?

If you are not asking yourself those questions routinely, you are at significant risk of being blindsided by events, and most likely at great cost.

Governance – living by the code

overnance is not something people think a great deal about; it mostly goes unnoticed, but it is in fact the glue that allows trust to exist in large social context. As societies got ever larger, the social rules became more complex and the means of managing people required processes that supported adherence to the rules. Governance is not the same as the law, but it can overlap the law. It can apply to how an organisation establishes processes to report on all its obligation, including its legal obligations. Parts of it may feel more like a code of conduct to ensure the intent of the law is followed.

There are many definitions of governance but essentially it is about the process an organisation puts into place to ensure it is adhering to its stated obligation. It is principally designed to inform management, shareholders, government, and community about its stated performance in being a good corporate citizen. If it's honest, it will also report on non-performance.

The Australian Institute of Company Directors define good governance as "... the effective way decisions are made, and power is exercised within an organisation"[31]. If you have a stated mission or corporate purpose, then it is about who is to be held accountable to effectively deliver on this stated purpose.

---

[31]https://www.aicd.com.au/good-governance.html

The reason for having governance is that the actions of a company have an incidental effect on society in which it is part. Being transparent creates the opportunity for trust.

Governance as an opportunity

Most would see governance as an imposition, a cost of doing business. But if you think on it a little more, it can actually deliver a great opportunity. One of the greatest challenges facing any organisation is how to create a valued organisation for its staff and customers. It begins with good governance and a willingness to accept that mistakes will happen, that owning up to errors is best. A culture of good governance and openness across the organisation means staff are confident there is transparency and that lies to cover things up are not culturally accepted. In the world of safety research, it is accepted that covering up or ignoring risk as a shortcut to 'getting things done' is mostly how accidents happen. If the staff value the openness of the organisations and its governance process, the customers will as well.

Establishing governance

At the highest-level, establishing governance is relatively straightforward, but as you get down into the details it becomes more nuanced and can at times become a little slippery. The most obvious place we are all familiar with is our local tax obligations, council regulations, state licences, and so forth. What is often more difficult is delivering on the public promises you are promoting around environmental responsibility, social responsibility, gender equity and the like. The former is a lot more punitive, so you may tend to pay them more attention, while the latter is more a "promise" but maybe not a "core promise[32]"?

---

[32] A "core promise" was part of political commentary in 2007 when the previous Australian Prime Minister invoke the term in which 'core promises' are those which he keeps in mind to hold traction for number crunching votes for the next federal election. A non-core promise were those he didn't intend to hold but were attractive to the electorates at the time.

This is where we come to the question of "intent" and trust. Governance is about a process that supports compliance around "intent." If we consider something like Fringe Benefit Tax, we all know the intent, and yet decades later we still hear people plead ignorance or confusion on the subject. Perhaps the details can at times confuse but the intent was always clear as can be. There is business expense – this is *claimable*, there is personal entertainment while on business – this is *not claimable*, and there is business entertainment – this is *claimable under FBT*. It's pretty simple, and deep down we all know it, but sometimes it seems people choose to forget, or feign confusion. The main thing that would avoid any confusion is to focus on the "intent". The business should not be paying for your personal expenditure, similarly while entertaining a client may be a cost to the business, reporting it under FBT makes the expense less likely to be overdone.

If we put so much effort into dodging punitive measures like simple tax rulings, we should consider what is likely to be our response where there is no punitive measure and little policing to hold anyone accountable. If corrupt practices, even small ones, are allowed to flourish, where does the trust end up? Is it really just bending the rules, or is it a gradual corrupting of the rules meant to support good intent? You want to be trusted; you must put concerted effort into delivering intent.

Assuming you have processes in place for your legal obligations, we also suggest you make a list of what, as an organisation, you stand for, and what are the processes you need in place to demonstrate that you are living up to those values? If you claim to be environmentally responsible, how are you going to demonstrate that you are? What processes do you have in place to support such a statement? This is especially important if your customers are relying on such statements to make purchasing or investment decisions, lest it comes under scrutiny as misleading.

To provide a structure to governance, businesses need to consider how decisions are made. Whether it is a single business owner, an informal family executive, a formal executive process, or a board. The underlying reason that's important is because the less people you have making all the decisions around governance, the more likely it is that poor practices will go unchallenged. You need to have a level of diversity to be able to cover all the skills required around environment and social obligations. This is not only a potential failure of small businesses but also of large corporations. In an article by Tensie Whelan from Harvard Business Review in January 2021 called *Boards are obstructing ESG - at Their Own Peril*, the author outlines that of the Fortune 100 companies in the US only about twenty nine percent had relevant ESG experience [33]. This would not be overly surprising if you have been to a director's course sometime in the last fifteen years. There, you would have experienced the strong emphasis on financial governance and not much on ESG. It simply wasn't on the radar at that time, but we suggest that the same level of diligence is required as you would with financials, but just on a different topic. Today the legacy of most boards are people who have a reasonably high level of financial literacy, but who for the most part have no qualifications around environment or social sciences. This stands in stark contrast to the market need for strong ESG credential from corporates. We can expect this to change as courses will increasingly have to consider ESG in their training. For SMEs, the more you can include a diverse set of views the less likely you are to blunder into an unexpected disaster, and if you do, you will be more likely to have a plan to extricate yourself. We have all seen how difficult this is to do when you look at the failed behaviour of large corporations. Who could forget the lack of independent oversight that led to the continuance of Madoff Investment Securities in the United States? A situation that led to one of the world's largest Ponzi schemes, worth over $60 billion until its collapse in 2008. What started as a small lie

---

[33]Whelan, T., 2021, *Boards Are Obstructing ESG - at Their Own Peril*. Harvard Business Review - Sustainable Business Practices.

with a small unknown investment broker escalated over decades into a complex fraudulent scheme that cost a great many people their life savings.

Tim Watts (IA Research) produced an interesting paper on *A Report on Corporate Governance at Five Companies that Collapsed in 2001*[34] . Here are some of the key points to keep in mind:

Ownership structure showed that 60% of failed companies had a single shareholder with effective control. Why is that important? IA Research argue that with effective control, the dominant shareholder can bypass the normal checks and balances, and processes of oversight that an effective board regularly uses to protect shareholders' interests.

Although founders of companies often have aligned interests with shareholders, they can also bring to their board duties several potential conflicts of interest and may have loyalties to the company history and reputation which may colour their judgement.

This suggest that the independence of directors is important to provide different perspectives and challenge vested interest. In the S&P/ASX 100, only 45% of directors are independent. What can happen is that when difficult decisions have to be made, but the board is dominated by directors with a vested interest in the current structure, there will naturally be inherent bias away from the hard but important restructuring decisions.

On another governance matter, choose your auditor carefully for independence. The role of the auditor is to provide trust with shareholders with an unbiased picture of the financial position of the company. Auditor independence is therefore crucial to the quality of the market's information about the performance and prospects of any company. Failed companies sometimes had the presence of personnel

---

[34]Watts, T. A, 2002, Report on Corporate Governance at Five Companies that Collapsed in 2001. Published by IA Research. IA research is a business of Institutional Analysis Pty Ltd. Melbourne. Email: info@ia.net.au.

from audit firms on their boards which draws into serious question the independence and overall quality of the audit information.

Having executive reward being contingent on performance was mostly lacking in failed companies. The higher the proportion of a CEO's remuneration that is "at risk", the more closely aligned are his or her interests with those of shareholders. If a CEO's pay doesn't fluctuate greatly between good and bad years, there is no tangible incentive for the CEO to make the changes necessary to improve overall company performance.

What IA Research conclude is that it is easy to put formal structures in place that enable all the relevant boxes to be ticked, with shareholders getting a false sense of security as a result. The real value is to demonstrate that your governance process doesn't just tick a process box but meets the intent of the organisation.

While this illustrates the way large corporation need to operate to manage governance, there are also important lessons for small businesses about the people you rely to inform you about how the business is performing.

For example, a Tasmanian woman has pleaded guilty to stealing $940,000 from her employer to fund her addiction to an online gambling game that does not pay out real money. She stole the money while working as an account manager at a Tasmanian small business between 2016 and 2019. It was only after she was made redundant in 2019 that "anomalies were discovered in banking transactions" and a further investigation revealed the full extent of her theft[35].

Making it fit the size of your business

When it comes to processes, size matters. The intent in developing a process is to ensure that your business purpose is reflected across all your business functions and staff are clear on your purpose. Whatever

---

[35]McDonald, L. 2021. Woman who stole $940k from employer left gambling app on auto while she slept. ABC News accessed 10/06/2023.

way you put it, somewhere either on the web, social media, or bill-boards, you will be saying something about not only what you are offer-ing as products and services, but who you are and what you stand for. That's all very well, providing your actions support your words.

Small organisations find it easier to create a homogenous work cul-ture, and management is generally more accessible. Communication is easier and more direct. As your organisation increases in size, it is likely your brand is going further afield, and this means you have more people to bring into the ethos of the organisation. You therefore need a level of process to record and account for everyone's action. This may seem daunting but not getting this right will have social consequences.

The thing to consider is that, unless staff are guided, they will inter-pret the business requirement in their own way. But neither can you be overly prescriptive, as it doesn't work in all situations. There has to be an element of judgement, and this is best guided by the culture you've established in your business. This is a tricky balance for management, but what works well is leading by example. If you don't live up to your rhetoric, staff will be disillusioned and find workarounds that suit them without you knowing. The 'not-knowing' is what will ultimately damage your brand. When things go wrong, the 'not-knowing' part is not a good look for management. There are many examples of this around the safety literature; see, for example, articles by Hale and Borys, 2013[36].

Organisational culture can be formally stated or informally under-stood. Having it formally stated is worth the effort; it tells staff not only what their job is but how to go about doing it. A company objective should be broad enough to allow some leeway for on-the-ground judge-ment, but clear in its intent. Sometimes intent needs to be reinforced. You could do worse than involve your staff in the process.

Where corporate strategy often fails is where the business objective is a parenthood statement that is ambiguous and difficult for staff to

---

[36]Hale, A. & Borys, D. 2013. Working to rule or working safely? Part 2: The management of safety rules and procedures. *Safety Science* 55(2013) 222-231. Elsevier publication.

interpret. Mission statements can sometimes be too long, want to do too much, or be made up of confusing corporate speak. Falsely worded objectives simply confuse staff who must make the everyday judgement about how they are delivering to this.

Measuring and reporting

Governance isn't so much about collecting data to promote yourself, but more about tracking your business function in all key areas, much the same as you do financially. It allows the business to understand when and where it needs to act.

Measuring and reporting is primarily about the numbers around what you do, such as staffing, and energy and water use. It's important to know the numbers you have about gender equality and sustainability, regardless of the size of your operation. The numbers need to tell a simple story. Governance is about collecting and keeping track of those numbers so you can report on them when required. The use of graphs, technical jargon, and tables are all very well, but they must be clear. Reporting is telling the story of what your organisation is doing in an honest and transparent way. You have to collect enough information over time, so the reporting does not lack important details. But also, be selective about what information you collect; overdoing it can be confusing. You might decide to track your energy consumption or community engagement. You can use a short form infographic presentation to outline what you are doing in any specific space. We are all aware you can simply select specific sets of data that supports your view. The problem with that is, if it doesn't reflect reality, sooner or later this will become obvious. It's important that any data you collect is detailed enough to give you a picture of the issues with confidence, but not so much as to be confusing. It is a balancing act. If something isn't right, you could look at the means of fixing it. Ignoring something doesn't make it go away.

The flip side of poor reporting is turning it into an obsession. This is where process people make reporting way bigger than it needs to be. They often lose sight of why you are reporting and what the key things you want to report on are. Some people just love data - the more the better in their view. If you collect a whole lot of data that is not very useful for reporting but to have it there, 'just in case', just remember there is a significant cost to doing this work. In summary, focus on the key things you want to say about your business and make sure you have the data in place to back what you claim. Think also about why you want to make those claims or what are the reporting items you are being asked by a customer.

Diversity in hiring

Equal opportunity for employment begins with the hiring process. Diversity, whether we are talking about gender, age, religious belief, or race is highly relevant to a business. Talent is agnostic of those demographics; if you want the best talent you can afford, then limiting the pool of applicants is a long-term cost. For example, Sodexo, a global-services company, analysed data from 50,000 managers across 90 entities around the world, and the results are compelling. They report that teams with a male–female ratio between 40 and 60 percent produce results that are more sustained and predictable than those of unbalanced teams[37]. Turban, Wu and Zhang (2019) in a Harvard Business Review article suggest that it works best where it is normative and accepted as part of the culture of the organisation[38].

There may be circumstances where your ability to balance genders would be limited, such as a small business. Similarly, some industry sectors simply do not have the gender balance on the supply side of the

---

[37]Landel, M., 2015, Gender balance and the link to performance. *McKinsey Quarterly,* February 1 2015 issue. McKinsey & Company publication.

[38]Turban, S., Wu, D. and Zhang, L. 2019, Research: When Gender Diversity Makes Firms More Productive. *Harvard Business Review*, February 11, 2019.

labour market. The key point is that if you want the best talent, you have to overcome any confirmation bias you may have, be it gender, race, or age.

Alongside this debate, the question of diversity 'quotas' inevitably rears its head. To have, or not to have quotas? It could be argued quotas go against applying the "best person for the job" principle. But quotas can also be important for providing an objective that makes you work at it. It is there primarily to challenge your confirmation bias about what is best for the business. If it's not a real goal but an 'aspirational' goal, you could argue it's likely to drop off the radar with so much else to do. No one expects a goal to happen immediately, but it focuses your attention to making it work in the longer term. If you are serious about it, you put in a quota as an objective and you work at it over time. The aim is to be aware of your unconscious bias. The appointment process can easily be biased, such as pushing non-negotiable working hours or the need to travel that does not favour parents with school age children. You may not succeed perfectly using a quota, but you have committed yourself to making it happen. If you see it as a future benefit and not an imposition, then it's normal commercial practice to make such improvements for the staff supporting your business.

Equity in the workplace

In regard to staff, there is a need for the application of fair principles. That means a level of equal pay for work that has the same level of responsibility. There may be payment bands based on experience, but they should not be disproportionate. Another principle is creating the same level of opportunity for all staff. To make this work, you as a manager need to let go of any preconceived idea about such things as gender roles or stereotyping. Making that paradigm shift in yourself is the first step. Changing the culture of an organisation must come from the executive level and it needs to be followed up and reinforced.

A level of inequality can certainly creep in over time, so it needs to be reviewed on occasions.

ESG is not telling organisations how they should run their business, but it does ask the question, are they providing their people the same opportunity? It is promoting the need for productive employment and decent work for all women and men, including for young people and persons with disabilities, and equal pay for work of equal value.

Transparency

Transparency is key to the ESG process. It is less about how well you did something and more about how open and honest you are about what worked and what didn't work so well. We are all aware that in most organisations, things don't always go to plan. You might have set a sustainability target or made some bold ambitious goals with the best of intentions, but circumstances didn't work out the way you had thought they would. In such circumstance, trying to hide the uncomfortable fact that you are not going to be able to meet your goal has risk written all over it. Why? Because it's hard to hide things for very long; not impossible, but very hard. This means eventually the truth will emerge and at that point your business trust is on the line because it might look as if you were being dishonest about your objective. If you are more upfront when things are not working, you will have a great deal more credibility.

While dodging an important topic investors and customers care about may not be smart, lying to hide something is worse. Lies, when uncovered, are hard to walk away from with your reputation intact. Anything you say after you are uncovered lying is suspect. To avoid such uncomfortable scrutiny, a spokesperson might use vague ambiguous language when questioned. You can do this simply by not answering the direct question but creating an answer to the 'question' you believe they should be asking. This strategy might work for a time but, at some point, stakeholders, whether customers or investors, will have a choice of action to make about your business.

In terms of advertising, there is a degree of public scepticism when people are looking at any claims made by businesses. If it is uncovered later that there was a lack of truth to your statements, then trust is lost. What it comes down to is, if you make a claim specifically to attract customers, is there the documentation to support those claims? Not everyone, but some, will question and dig a little deeper, and so will your competitors. Unless, of course, they are doing the same thing.

Where transparency ends, and commercial confidence begins, is one of those grey areas that can be confused. From an ESG perspective, transparency is about how you do business; being honest about your product capability, your community efforts, and how you treat your people and the environment. Your commercial IP can remain in complete confidence.

Sometimes what is termed commercial confidentiality is arbitrarily applied to mistakes that can hurt a business. A clerical error in over-charging for a service might be an example. This may result in owning up to mistakes being blocked not so much for 'commercial in confidence' reasons but to avoid executive embarrassment or awkward public questions. Too much of a shift towards lack of openness for the wrong reason and you lose the benefit of doing so in engendering trust. In the wash up, it is 'trust' that is at the heart of this concept.

Many of us are familiar with corporate financial transparency but less so with environmental and social credentials such as a product being sustainably sourced or carbon neutral. All ASX-listed companies[39] have reporting obligations, and as part of that reporting obligation they will document their financial position on their website. For small private companies, and even large private companies, this is not a requirement so you can tailor make this to suit your needs. If your advertising does make soft claims, you should outline how this is supported via documentation. Hard claims will obviously attract the attention of consumer affairs and are not a consideration in this discussion.

---

[39]ASX refers to the Australian Stock Exchange.

Spotting dodgy claims

As previously indicated, people are by nature a little bit sceptical, so they may not accept corporate or business statements at face value. Will most people pursue every claim for fact checking? Probably not, but they may suspend judgement until new information is presented. Dodgy claims are generally the ones that are a bit vague or involve the excessive use of cliches resorted by a lot of companies. The vagueness leaves a lot of room for different interpretation. Words like 'sustainability,' 'environmentally friendly' or 'we value people' are common and say precious little about how companies will do the things that would support such statements. Being more specific has considerably more credibility. If you, in some way, support an endangered species and explain how you do this, that has value and is verifiable. Similarly, demonstrating renewable electrification across the business is a verifiable environmental measure. More so if you can get endorsement by a credible third party such as a well-known non-profit organisation.

Another poor habit is virtue signalling by making statements that are not supported by internal actions. An example of virtue signalling is when an organisation flaunts their views, usually on social media, to make themselves look good in the eyes of the public. They post about participating in a charity event maybe without clearly doing anything tangible to support the cause. While declaring your corporate values is a good thing, it should be followed by tangible actions. Simply stating your support for diversity or disability employment areas is not enough if this is at much lower wages than is generally considered fair. It's important that your public opinion or statement is matched by real tangible action.

Lip service to consultation

Consultation is about listening, reflecting, and making changes accordingly. What we see with most community consultation, however, is an exercise in box ticking and using that as the green light for what you have already decided to do before the consultation. Sound familiar? It's quite easy to bias a consultative process as a result of where it's held, what time it's held, and how it was advertised. It's fair enough that you can't hold a meeting in every town in the country, but there are different ways of consulting that help, from webinars, interviews, and written submissions, as well as public meetings. Moreover, consultation doesn't always need to be formally organised by you. It may be as simple as listening at community forums, following social media, or simply asking questions in various settings.

We know we can do this well because when you change 'community consultation' to 'consumer focus group,' we pull out all stops to get it right.

Why would any organisation, public or private, consider stakeholder consultation? The answer is simple, it's to test your underlying assumptions. Having the wrong assumptions can create business risk and can cost you money when you have to address issues you got wrong or might simply have missed as an opportunity.

The ability to use different interviewing techniques is another way to obtain valuable information in developing organisational strategies. It is worth investigating interview techniques such as in-depth interviewing[40] or Convergent interviewing[41]. Whilst many would be aware of in-depth interviewing techniques, 'convergent interviewing' may be less well known. It is a qualitative technique of interviewing where questions are adapted on the go to refine the subject. Material from one expert on a subject can be shared with others for further comment and further refinement, until you have a strong sense of the subject.

---

[40]Victor Minichiello, Rosalie Aroni and Terrence Hays. 2008. *In-depth Interviewing: Principles, Techniques, Analysis*. Pearson Australia Group. Monash University.

[41]Wil Williams and Duncan Lewis. 2005. Convergent interviewing: a tool for strategic investigation. In the journal *Strategic Change* 14: 219-229 (2005). Wiley Interscience publication.

The principal value of consultation for businesses, in whatever form you choose to do it, is helping to develop strategies. This is particularly important where resources are most often limited, and you need to make choices on where to invest or better understand the risks and opportunities associated with a particular strategy. Most corporates use this via their sales staff, who not only deliver knowledge but are trained to gather customer intelligence along the way. Sometimes untrained sales staff can become overly focussed on targets and can forget that 'sales' is also a two-way information process and incoming intelligence can be very valuable to adapt management strategy.

Managing the need for change

Managing change is never easy. Everyone is rarely on the same page at the same time. But if owners and senior managers don't support change it does not happen, and if workers on the ground don't support change, it will be poorly implemented and may even backfire. Therefore, change takes whatever time it takes for everyone to get on board. It also needs purpose and investment.

Changing cultural attitudes needs leadership that recognises that established paradigms are hard to shift. Nowhere is this more apparent than the role of women in heavy industries or in traditionally male-oriented industries like the military or agriculture. The established paradigms have been difficult to shift, often taking decades, and statements of support for this by management have not always been sufficient. Often senior executives, mostly male, do not have first-hand experience of the issues on the ground for women. There are usually many layers of reporting in between. This means that the messages of support around the social issues are mostly crafted by staff more focussed on image than substance.

For SMEs with smaller staff numbers and greater transparency, this is an opportunity to shine and provide increased competitiveness. This doesn't just apply to gender but is applicable across the whole breadth of ESG. Large organisations have a lot of internal friction when it comes to making changes simply by virtue of having more people, with more resources invested in existing structures that support the status-quo. Smaller SMEs have greater agility to be able to harmonise culture and shift resources around.

For management, inertia is a big problem; they are so busy doing the everyday, they never get to see their organisation from the outside. Ever been to a shop or café and wonder why things don't seem to get fixed or look a bit shabby? It's most likely everyone is too focussed on the job at hand, that they no longer see the deteriorating or the unfinished bits. It's a bit like that with culture, we can miss things until it becomes an issue. Sometimes we need to step outside the business for a bit and look at things like someone new.

The problem with this inertia is that it blinds us to risk and opportunity. Most organisations have had to change and evolve over time; you can either look ahead and make those changes proactively or simply react to events.

Making governance standard operating procedure

In summary, governance rests at the heart of ESG and it is through governance that organisations can ensure that they don't fall into traps where action is out of step with intent. It's therefore important to make sure that it is applied properly. Make adhering to governance processes standard operating procedure throughout the organisation. This will help you avoid surprises, especially unpleasant ones. It will highlight where the resources need to be more strategically placed. It should be designed to help you have an open and honest look at your community responsibility and demonstrate where and how it needs to improve. A governance process should be open to change if it is not delivering on intent. This is key; it must not become one of those rules that nobody knows why it's there. Governance must always speak to the stated business purpose and intent.

You should not expect that this to be an overnight process, but rather an ongoing activity. Start in one corner and work your way across the organisation. It is certainly important to get step buy-in when developing agreed behaviours.

The United Nation Sustainability Goals

In the previous chapters we attempted to outline a big picture of what ESG is about, covering a whole range of issues around people and the environment. In this final chapter we will look at how you might contextualise it to your business. We will highlight a plan for an ESG program but only you can fill in the details to suit your particular business. ESG is not a compliance form you fill out, and we recommend that businesses need to understand the principles of sustainability before making statements.

How we might view what is meant by sustainability has already been considered by the United Nations. The Global Sustainable Development Report (GSDR) which originated in "The Future We Want," was the outcome of the Rio+20 conference that took place in Rio de Janeiro, Brazil, in June 2012 – marking twenty years after the landmark 1992 Earth Summit in Rio. Rio+20 was also an opportunity for the global community to look ahead to the world we want in 20 years. Member States at the time were laying the groundwork for the 2030 Agenda for Sustainable Development and the 17 associated Sustainable Development Goals (See Table 3). ESG then becomes the process of how you are supporting efforts towards those goals as individuals, businesses, and government.

TABLE 3: The 17 United Nations Sustainability goals

Goal 1	End poverty in all its forms everywhere
Goal 2	End hunger, achieve food security and improved nutrition and promote sustainable agriculture
Goal 3	Ensure healthy lives and promote well-being for all at all ages
Goal 4	Ensure inclusive and equitable quality education and promote lifelong learning opportunities for all
Goal 5	Achieve gender equality and empower all women and girls
Goal 6	Ensure availability and sustainable management of water and sanitation for all
Goal 7	Ensure access to affordable, reliable, sustainable and modern energy for all
Goal 8	Promote sustained, inclusive and sustainable economic growth, full and productive employment and decent work for all
Goal 9	Build resilient infrastructure, promote inclusive and sustainable industrialization and foster innovation
Goal 10	Reduce inequality within and among countries
Goal 11	Make cities and human settlements inclusive, safe, resilient and sustainable
Goal 12	Ensure sustainable consumption and production patterns
Goal 13	Take urgent action to combat climate change and its impacts*
Goal 14	Conserve and sustainably use the oceans, seas and marine resources for sustainable development
Goal 15	Protect, restore and promote sustainable use of terrestrial ecosystems, sustainably manage forests, combat desertification, and halt and reverse land degradation and halt biodiversity loss

Goal 16	Promote peaceful and inclusive societies for sustainable development, provide access to justice for all and build effective, accountable and inclusive institutions at all levels
Goal 17	Strengthen the means of implementation and revitalize the global partnership for sustainable development

It should be emphasised that this is a global aspiration and therefore some of the goals may look unrelated to circumstances in the Global North including Australia. If you think of your business as part of the global community, then you will see there is a role that you can play. These global goals are the starting point for your ESG statement.

Under each goal is a series of more detailed targets. Consider what you might already be doing in meeting the targets set out. For example:

Goal 7 - Ensure access to affordable, reliable, sustainable and modern energy for all.

The targets under goal 7 include (not a complete list):

7.1 - By 2030, ensure universal access to affordable, reliable, and modern energy services

7.2 - By 2030, increase substantially the share of renewable energy in the global energy mix

7.3 - By 2030, double the global rate of improvement in energy efficiency.

If you are transitioning a component of your business to renewable energy either by purchasing green energy or investing in solar panels, you are effectively contributing to goal 7.2.

Under each of the targets is a series of indicators such as:

7.2.1 - Renewable energy share in the total final energy consumption

This means your share of renewable energy as a percentage is increasing relative to the total final energy consumption. The targets do not set a 'number target' as situations are highly variable. Obviously 100% would be ideal but that may not always be possible, but you can report on your contribution.

Because ESG is a process that can cover so many things under the United Nations sustainability goals, and given resources are limited, you are going to have to make some choices about what you can manage and what you want to report on. This is going to be different for every business. Some businesses are going to be under a great deal more pressure than others.

The meaning behind sustainability is simple, it's about the long-term survival of the business in a way that does not harm the resources it relies on. There is a limit to natural resources. If we don't change the way we use these natural resources and the way we do business, we will all pay the price at some future date. An example is over-fishing of certain species; if it's not controlled, the populations crashes and everybody loses. The bottom line is that we need, as a minimum, access to fresh water, nutritious food, clean air, and a climate that can support life. If only some of us have those things but others not, there will be conflict. Those basics do not really come on our radar until we do not have them. Businesses thrive on the basis of stability and having sufficient resources, including human resources. Ecological economists have been warning us for some time that there are limits to industrial growth in trying to accommodate a planet of 8 billion people and growing.

Changes of fortune for businesses as a result of climate change are the not the same everywhere. Some areas will thrive while others will languish. The question for most small business owners is whether they can pivot in time before they are outcompeted. How you compete while still supporting the principles of sustainability is one of those deciding factors; not the only one, but an important one. This is because surviving on less customers due to competition means you have less altitude to manoeuvre. On the other hand, small businesses have a certain agility to be able to win back customers around sustainability that big business cannot do quickly. ESG holds both risks and opportunities for small business and learning about ESG early minimises the risk.

It is worth taking some time out to reflect on how you want your business to be seen by customers. This is about being strategic, not tactical. Consider what will survival look like 10 years from now? Obviously, no one can predict future markets beyond an educated guess, however it is worth being informed about current trends that may impact future markets. We can see that a number of current resources, for example timber supplies, are under demand pressure and this will require a sustainability plan as part of the supply chain. The greater the disruption to supply chains, the greater the public disquiet and the more focus it brings to the need for change. We are seeing this from drought, floods, heat waves, and a whole host of climate events. Let us consider these key environmental elements for business risk.

As we consider ESG reporting, we will look more closely at the issues around some of the 17 UN sustainability goals and dive deeper into various elements of environment and social issues.

We will begin with the key environmental elements of sustainability as it applies to Australia and their importance to business.

The future of freshwater is covered by goal 6 - Ensure availability and sustainable management of water and sanitation for all.

Freshwater is critical to survival for all organisms. It's also critical to any business, and it can be taken for granted until there is an acute supply shortage. This is evident during periods of prolonged drought. A community has an expectation that you will be respectful of how you use and treat freshwater. When it comes to freshwater, there is mostly too little or too much, especially in Australia. Climate change and growing population demand will likely magnify those extremes of flood and droughts. We cannot tell you how much and how long, the only sure thing is more extremes, and more unpredictability.

According to the Intergovernmental Panel on Climate Change, water shortages are likely to increase globally in the next few decades, as more people compete for limited surface-water supplies[42]. Ground water is also not the answer as many aquafers are gradually being depleted. For a business, this will increase scrutiny on how water is managed. It is also likely that the cost to access water is going to go up, and we have already seen this upward trend for irrigators. We are talking in decade terms here. Given that planning, resourcing, and changes in water infrastructure is a long-term investment, now is a good time to start to evaluate your freshwater needs for the future and how you can minimise any harmful outflow.

The future of food is covered by goal 2 - End hunger, achieve food security and improved nutrition and promote sustainable agriculture.

As the population increases, demand is expected to increase accordingly. If you are in the food supply chain, several things will become apparent over time. Firstly, the cost of food production is increasing via input costs and consumers are not accounting for maintenance of the farm's natural resource in the price the farmers are paid for their produce. Secondly, there is growing global demand, but rapidly escalating food costs are going to severely impact the poorest demographic. There is a two-part demand; the basic staples of grain access for the poorest people and increasing demand for high-value animal protein for those areas with increasing incomes. Nutritional levels are not globally equal. Thirdly, this wealth inequality is fostering excess waste at

---

[42]Andersen, I. 2021. Climate change, water scarcity and security. Pre-COP 26 event on 'Water Security Under Climate Change' hosted by the University of Glasgow. United Nations, Environment Programme.

one end and acute shortages at the other end. This disparity in food availability is quite staggering!

In terms of ESG, there are limitations as to what most businesses can do, as they may not be directly involved or have a great deal of control over the food supply chain. They can, however, ensure that they are not contributing to food waste, where possible ensuring the sustainability of farm suppliers, and looking at innovative ways to support those suffering acute shortages of food. They are a number of charities that will collect food that may be going to waste. If you are catering for work events, of course you don't want to under-cater, but why not put a plan in place for leftover food rather than put it into landfill?

A lot of food is thrown out for cosmetic reasons. According to the OzHarvest organisation, one third of all food produced is lost, which is around 1.3 billion tonnes of food – costing the global economy close to $940 billion each year[43]. That's a staggering amount of food given that the World Health organisation reports as many as 828 million people were affected by hunger in 2021. You might feel you cannot solve this global dilemma, but you can certainly do your bit to not contribute to the problem.

The future of clean air is covered by goal 3 - Ensure healthy lives and promote well-being for all at all.

Clean is a relative term. As living breathing mammals, a certain level of oxygen relative to other gases is necessary. Certain other gases, about 50 of them, are life-limiting, such as carbon monoxide, hydrogen sulphide, and chlorine. Clean, from our point of view, is not having gases that create either chronic or acute conditions. Some of those gases are a natural part of earth systems, but we don't need to add to them industrially as well. Industrial pollutant has long been under scrutiny and that pressure is likely to continue, especially in major cities. You

---

[43]OzHarvest, 2023. Food Waste Fact. At ozharvest.org/food-waste-facts. Accessed 11/06/2023.

may not be a large industrial polluter, but it might be worth checking your contribution in the supply chain.

Increasing demand for industrial products is going to demand ways of reducing atmospheric pollution affecting health directly. This has broader economic implications for governments, who are likely to increase pressure on industry to reduce their impact on human health. Some of those impacts could be a future risk for you as part of a supply chain. Reducing the burning of fossil fuel by turning to alternative, cleaner energy sources, is certainly an area that business can minimise air pollution and at the same time save money.

The future of shelter is covered by goal 11 - Make cities and human settlements inclusive, safe, resilient and sustainable.

As animals go, humans are fragile and require shelter to survive. We pour a lot of resources into shelter. On occasions, extravagantly so. In Australia we are leading the world in household floor space per capita and getting bigger. According to the real estate industry, the average size of a new Australian house increased from 162.2 square metres to 227.6 square metres between 1984 and 2003, that's a jump of 40%[44]. This means greater demand on building resources. However, occupation of these bigger houses has gone from 4.5 people in 1911 to 2.6 in 2011, and the average number of persons per household remained stable at 2.6 as at the 2022 census. So, it's not about bigger families needing more space, but most places having more rooms, many of which are not occupied. According to the Australian Bureau of Statistics data on housing utilisation over this same period, the number of single-person households increased from 19% to 29% in 2018 and steadied at 26% in 2022[45]. The upshot, we have less people in bigger, more expen-

---

[44]Sorensen, E. 2017 - Why are our houses getting bigger? Article by Realestate.com.au

[45]Australian Bureau of Statistics, 2022. Housing: Census Information on housing type and housing costs.' Reference period 2021. Released 28/06/2022

sive houses. Is the trend indicating a potential for a correction given the increasing cost and limited resources available such as timber? Business premises are likewise going through a correction post-Covid lockdowns. According to an ABC article by Melissa Maykin (August 2022), data from the Property Council of Australia indicated that new commercial occupancy rates fell across almost every major Australian city during the month of June [46]. Will that trend continue? It's hard to be sure but it has changed the office working paradigm for many workers and that could well flow on to commercial construction. From the perspective of ESG, office space, like housing space, demands resources. If businesses can find innovative ways of maintaining or improving work performance but use less resources this is an important contribution to environment.

In a world with limited resources and increasing costs, it is likely that space utilisation will come under closer scrutiny.

The future of fibre is covered by goal 12 - Ensure sustainable consumption and production patterns.

Modern society has built a whole industry around this. Our actual need for fibre is not overly high but we have made it so. We have invested a great deal of our emotion in the need for updating our fashion accessories using fibre goods such as clothing, linen, and furniture. Based on present demand, synthetic fibres are the most-produced type of fibre and make up close to two thirds of all fibre production, with natural fibres just under a third, and cellulosic fibres at around 5%. Polyester is the most produced individual fibre of all fibres (approximately 65 million tonnes in 2017) and cotton is the most consumed natural fibre (81%)[47,48].

---

[46]Makin, M. 2022. CBD commercial occupancy rates have fallen across the country — so what will it take to get workers back into city offices? ABC online.

[47]Statista.com report. *Production volume of chemical and textile fibers worldwide from 1975 to 2021.* Industry provider of market and consumer data.

[48]Dnfi.org - *Discover Natural Fibres Initiative* is a cotton industry data platform. Sourced April 2023.

Consumption is mostly dominated by the G7 countries, as well as Korea, Switzerland, Taiwan, and Australia.

The dilemma for consumers is that polyester is based on oil, and cotton takes up land and water. They have excellent fibre quality hence the demand and likelihood of their increasing market demand into the future. There is no doubt that fibre production in the future will depend on various factors, such as the supply and price of feedstocks such as petrochemicals (with petroleum/oil being a feedstock for polyester), and the yields of plants like cotton for natural fibres. There is also an argument about land resource competition of fibre and biofuels versus food production. The simple economic reality is that best returns/hectare tend to win the day, as long as the demand is there.

At this point, consumer demand is having little impact on production and certainly that could change over time but is not expected to happen quickly. This is driven by low relative cost and a disposable fashion culture.

By 2030, fibre demand is forecasted to be close to 70 million tons for polyester and just over 30 million tons for cotton. Other fibre types based on cellulose are gaining ground but only slowly[49].

The future of key minerals is covered across a range of goals.

Another simple reality is that the components of a renewable industry demand a great deal of earth resources. According to the United States Geological Survey in 2019, photovoltaic cells require arsenic, gallium, germanium, indium, and tellurium. Wind turbines need aluminium and other rare earth metals. Batteries need lithium, graphite, cobalt, and manganese. There is also a need for tungsten, molybdenum, antimony, and more[50]. Not to mention the need for iron and concrete in

---

[49]Textileworld.com

[50]United State Geological Survey. Critical Mineral Commodities in Renewable Energy. 2019

the supply chain. If you have never heard of some of these elements, you are not alone. Unless you have a chemistry major or are a big fan of the periodic table, it's unlikely you would have come across these elements. Many are rare and limited in supply, reliant on a small number of countries. Fortunately, Australia is well placed to supply a number of these key minerals[51].

For small businesses, expect that increasing global demand and limited supply is going to keep the capital cost of renewable energy infrastructure up for quite some time. Supply is also likely to be impacted by any geopolitical turmoil. It may not follow the expected trend that things will simply get cheaper with time.

Mapping the United Nations ENVIRONMENTAL Sustainability Goals

There are several other goals that support the environmental space, noting that some will overlap with social areas. We will only concentrate on the ones that are more applicable to Australia. The full details are covered by the United Nations website. The environmental goals include:

GOAL 7 - Ensure access to affordable, reliable, sustainable, and modern energy for all.

This goal, used earlier as an example, is about improving global access to efficient, renewable energy. Increasingly, business and institutions are turning to investing in renewable energy, primarily to save cost, but also to support customer needs. This is notable in community infrastructure in rural regions using micro-grids as well as the increasing use of rooftop solar. Apart from renewable energy infrastructure, there is also support for energy efficiency through better insulation and options to reduce urban heat islands such as the provision of shade and choosing

---

[51]Cenki, B. 2020. *Critical minerals are vital for renewable energy, we must learn to mine them responsibly.* Published in The Conversation February 17, 2020.

reflective colours in heat-prone areas. The advantage most businesses have compared to individuals is access to capital for modernising infrastructure, and for many operators, electricity demand is at its highest during daylight hours.

Target 7.2 looks to substantially increase the share of renewable energy in the global energy mix by 2030. If you have the capital and you own your premises, this makes sense as your energy demands tend to coincide with daylight hours and available solar energy.

Target 7.3 looks to double the global rate of improvement in energy efficiency by 2030. Once again this makes sense for businesses given the increasing cost of energy.

So, Goal 7 should be a clear winner for most businesses, but only if you own the premises and have access to capital.

GOAL 9 – Build resilient infrastructure, promote inclusive and sustainable industrialization, and foster innovation.

The engineers in the room will love this one. This is about making infrastructure more resilient, more environmentally efficient, and fit for purpose. This could be something like making your building or workshop more energy efficient. Given the increasing cost of energy this is a go to for many businesses, the most obvious being solar panels. You could also look at reducing heat emission and managing water quality. More imaginatively, you could increase green spaces to sequester carbon and increase oxygen. Given our technological capability this is a serious consideration for many businesses as a win-win.

GOAL 12 – Ensure sustainable consumption and production patterns.

This is about reducing waste and unnecessary over-consumption, supporting recycling and better practices that cuts areas of waste. Reuse or repurpose. There are many areas of businesses where a proactive approach in this space helps reduce waste but can also reduce cost. This would be a good time to look at your waste stream and see if it has a value to someone else or can it be repurposed in some way. A number of businesses have turned their waste into an add-on business. For example, bagasse, a waste from sugar cane crushing, is now converted into a range of biomass feed stocks including "drop-in" fuels that can be tailored to use as jet fuel or diesel, as well as bio-based plastics[52].

Target 12.2 wants to achieve the sustainable management and efficient use of natural resources by 2030. From a business perspective, it makes sense to reduce natural resource cost inputs such as water.

If you happen to be in the right industry, Target 12.3 is looking to halve per capita global food waste at the retail and consumer levels, and reduce food losses along production and supply chains, including post-harvest losses. Reducing food waste is something many businesses can play a role in.

Often, waste can be a resource if you look into it deeply enough. At the very least make sure waste is minimised, which supports Target 12.5 that wants to substantially reduce waste generation through prevention, reduction, recycling, and reuse. The indiscriminate use of plastic is a major issue, given that less than a quarter of plastic waste is actually recyclable. In 2023, legislation in the UK will ban single-use items such as plastic cutlery, plates, and trays, along with previously banned single-use plastic straws, stirrers, and cotton buds in a bid to reduce pollution. Such measures are becoming increasingly common across the developed world. A number of large corporations have indicated that managing plastic use in their supply chain is on their radar.

There are eight global targets under sustainable consumption, and many of them will have positive profit implications as well as contributing to social and environmental good.

---

[52]Groves, m. 2021. *Pilot plant turning sugarcane waste into jet fuel, diesel, plastics prepares to flick switch.* Article on ABC Rural.

GOAL 13 – Take urgent action to combat climate change and its impacts.

This is arguably the goal most businesses are currently focussed on. There is already a great deal of literature on managing this through reducing emissions and sequestering carbon. Certainly, every business can have a role in firstly understanding their source of greenhouse gas emissions, and secondly looking at ways to reduce it. You might also want to consider adaptive measures given the time it might take to reduce greenhouse gas emissions. Given how prominent this issue has been, we will assume that this action requirement is already well known to you, so will leave it up to you for now.

GOAL 14 – Conserve and sustainably use the oceans, seas, and marine resources for sustainable development.

An important goal for those in coastal catchments to consider is how their practices might be affecting our marine environment. Eliminating plastic waste and improving the outflow of water quality to the ocean are two important examples. There is also a role around the greening of the supply chain that is connected to marine resources.

Target 14.1 aims to prevent and significantly reduce marine pollution of all kinds, in particular from land-based activities, including marine debris and nutrient pollution. For those working in the marine environment it may also be about educating your clients who may not be that knowledgeable about marine ecosystems. These ecological systems are complex and not always well understood by the public with limited marine interaction.

Many of the other targets around sustainable fishing, ocean acidification, marine research, and reef restoration are more government policy areas or for specialist organisations. You can, however, contribute financially to supporting the protection of important habitat areas.

GOAL 15 - Protect, restore, and promote sustainable use of terrestrial ecosystems, sustainably manage forests, combat desertification, halt and reverse land degradation, and halt biodiversity loss.

This is an area we can all have a role to play, given we are terrestrial and by necessity we have a land footprint. If we cannot do anything ourselves directly, can we support others in reducing deforestation and improving biodiversity. There is as much to do here in Australia to protect existing biodiverse areas and options for reforestation. Given this is a global problem, it is not surprising that there are a lot of UN targets related to this goal.

Target 15.1 is about ensuring the conservation, restoration, and sustainable use of terrestrial and inland freshwater ecosystems and their services, in particular forests, wetlands, mountains, and drylands. 15.2 is to promote the implementation of sustainable management of all types of forests, halt deforestation, restore degraded forests, and substantially increase afforestation[53] and reforestation. 15.3 is asking us to do what we can to combat desertification and restore degraded land. 15.4 is to cover conservation of mountain ecosystems, including their biodiversity. 15.5 is more generally about reducing the degradation of natural habitats, halt the loss of biodiversity, and prevent the extinction of threatened species. There is more, but we think you understand the picture.

There are two ways a business can approach this - one is directly help with protecting habitats and regenerating natural habitats, or the other is supporting organisations whose expertise it is to protect and restore natural habitats. That support can be in the way of funding or encouraging customers to support you in doing this. For most with limited resources the latter is probably more appropriate.

---

[53]Afforestation is the establishment of a forest in previously deforested areas. Afforestation programs aim to create forests and increase carbon capture and is mainly done for conservational and commercial purposes.

Mapping the United Nations SOCIAL Sustainability Goals

If you imagine your business as a "person" in the community, then that role comes with social obligations. Your business has rights, but with those rights comes responsibility. Under the social sustainability goals there are several UN targets that speak to those obligations. Some of the goals are the province of governments and will not be covered in detail here.

GOAL 1 – End poverty in all its forms everywhere

While poverty at the level described by the UN is less likely to be evident in Australia, it does not mean that there are not abhorrent levels of poverty in parts of Australia. As a business, do you have something to contribute to reduce poverty in your community? We know resources for housing and cost of living is really stretching members of our own community, so supporting charitable institutions is a good start.

The most important relevance this has to ESG is sourcing suppliers that provide fair wages and work conditions. Businesses have started asking suppliers about the sustainability conditions from which their product has been derived. We will see an increasing role in reporting the provenance of goods.

GOAL 2 – End hunger, achieve food security and improved nutrition, and promote sustainable agriculture.

Nutrition and agriculture are specialist areas and may not suit many businesses. But there are things one can do to promote healthy eating and encourage the development of a sustainable supply chain. Reach into your supply chain to see if it's relevant for you to support sustainable practices. Do you have knowledge and experience that can support this goal?

GOAL 3 – Ensure healthy lives and promote well-being for all at all ages.

This is strongly in the health sector, reducing infant mortality, the spread of human diseases like AIDS, and minimising drug abuse and accidents. For Australian businesses a lot is covered under established Occupational Health and Safety laws. Areas that may be more discretionary to businesses are staff mental health, the provision of carer's leave, sponsoring staff gym membership, or the provision of free flu shots.

GOAL 4 – Ensure inclusive and equitable quality education and promote lifelong learning opportunities for all.

This goal is focused on supporting youth education opportunities in low socio-economic areas. This can help businesses recruit a future workforce, with the aim being education helps create good citizens. The majority of support is usually targeted at sponsoring educational material or supporting construction of education facilities. If you have access to certain resources or have knowledge of this area, is there some way in which you can contribute?

GOAL 5 – Achieve gender equality and empower all women and girls.

This is about the support for gender equity in all its forms and taking action to reduce the disadvantage experience by many women. This is more acute in some countries than others but the fact that it is a goal in its own right is indicative of its chronic presence across all cultures, including in Australia. We would suggest that this should be part of corporate culture as standard practice. It is part of our legal system, but it also needs be supported at a social level.

GOAL 6 – Ensure availability and sustainable management of water and sanitation for all.

Maintaining the quality of water catchments isn't only an environmental responsibility, but a social obligation. In terms of businesses, as with any member of the community we should be conscious not to waste potable water. Prolonged droughts have highlighted that the availability of clean fresh water is not always guaranteed. A number of regional towns have seen their water storages run to near empty requiring water to be transported. It is incumbent on businesses not to waste drinking water.

GOAL 8 – Promote sustained, inclusive and sustainable economic growth, full and productive employment and decent work for all.

In Australia, this is principally covered by established labour laws in most cases. It is mostly about having an inclusive workforce, and fair pay and working conditions. You want to be sure that your international supply chain is adhering to these principles as well. Businesses can additionally lead by example by being inclusive in offering employment opportunities.

GOAL 10 – Reduce inequality within and among countries.

This is a more internationally focused agenda, and may be difficult for small to medium enterprises not involved in international trade. Essentially, it is about having the same sort of fair dealings with internationals as you would consider locally. It is asking us not to exploit the vulnerability of developing countries. For the most part, the main action for small businesses will be about being informed about their supply chain and the manner in which what they purchased has been made. Be especially careful of cheap goods that are the results of slave labour in developing countries.

This might also cover supporting people with disabilities with more appropriate facilities. Many businesses simply do not have suitable facilities for those that require wheelchair access.

UN sustainability goals & governance

The UN goals do not see governance as a specific goal but relies on it as an ethos of social justice. The most explicit example is Goal 16, which is to promote peaceful and inclusive societies for sustainable development, provide access to justice for all, and build effective, accountable, and inclusive institutions at all levels.

There is a role that everyone can play in terms of governance, and that is ensuring ethical practices and transparency to avoid corruption. While some practices such as collusion are covered under ASIC[54], there are grey areas that, while legal, may be considered unethical. Doing the right thing and to be seen to be doing the right thing, provides a long-term benefit for both the community as well as the business.

Making choices

It's clear that mapping the UN sustainability goals to your business is large and complex. It is important to consider that the targets are global. You can only contribute a part, but if you do even a small part it helps everyone. If you reduce a small amount of waste, it benefits all. If you support the protection of a habitat, it benefits all. You are the conscience of the business - what can the business achieve without endangering its long-term future? Your participation should be carefully considered so you are able to confidently say 'this will be our part.' As you look you around, you will see hundreds of businesses doing the same. It is not without effort, but businesses like people are judged on their behaviour.

Consideration for allocating resources

Action comes with a cost; so, the next stage is to consider the risk and benefits of any particular action. The difficulty will always be that

---

[54]ASIC is the Australian Securities and Investment Commission, a government body responsible for regulating Australia's markets and financial services.

future risks or benefits are difficult to predict. However, given that taking action now has an immediate cost, but with the benefits only to be delivered in the future, we recognise this has uncertainty similar to any other investment.

One of the most obvious sustainable actions for business is around energy. Renewable energy investment has an immediate capital cost, plus a maintenance and replacement timeline. Parts of the technology (e.g., solar panels) are now mature and much more affordable, but have no reliability at night, whereas batteries provide reliability of service, but early costs are high. A business also must consider energy storage alternatives, cost of capital, efficacy, and future changes in price and maintenance. Supply chain disruption (e.g., geopolitical events) can make future parts unavailable or overly expensive but can also change the economics compared to current energy sources. An example is the price of gas. Given future events are unpredictable, calculations can only be made based on current projections.

The example above involves a fairly standard capital investment decision and is usually well within the province of most businesses to manage.

A less obvious example is supply-chain analysis for sustainability indicators. This is an analysis that goes beyond the normal cost of supplier reliability to one that deals with sustainable provenance. The main cost of doing this is labour; it's a big job and needs a human with good social skill. It's not as straight forward as simply interrogating your supplier, it's a delicate matter. The 'against' is potential relationship cost, the benefit is that you have an answer when you are asked for similar information by your corporate customer or your financial provider. If you find things are not kosher with your supplier, you are going to have to consider some form of transition, and that cannot happen quickly.

If, for example, you allocate staff or consultants to review your supply chain backwards as part of your product life cycle analysis, it may change the cost of your product. It may also be a catalyst for change in a more substantial way. Either way, you will have a clearer picture of whether the goods you produce or the services you offer has a future. If you are going to be pushed by your competitor, you need to know the new rules at play. No one is going to volunteer to tell you if you are becoming uncompetitive; you will only know when it's happened. This is about understanding the true cost of your product and allowing it to be priced accordingly.

Another option is supporting the community or what the community cares about. If it's obvious that your activity has some degree of inevitable environmental damage, you can offset this by supporting a benefit elsewhere, providing they are equitable. It's not just about the cost of offset that is important but the degree of transparency and fairmindedness you bring to the equation. Resources are always limited so it pays to carefully choose the project that best suits the business, rather than go for what's popular.

Reporting and messaging

There is two parts to ESG reporting, one is the detailed internal reporting that measures progress, and the other is external reporting, which is usually in the form of an executive summary and tends to be light on details. Obviously, they need to match.

We need to start with the details first, because, unless you are clear on the facts, it's risky to make public statements. It is certainly important for boards and management to be reassured that the facts support the statements. The format is not as critical as having confidence that statements can be supported with facts. If the facts are not categorical, then the assumptions underpinning your conclusion should be made clear.

Before you embark on a ESG program or project you must have a sound methodology. A methodology is all the details about how things are to be done, how the project is to be measured (metrics), and how bias has been managed. It should be repeatable in the way of a scientific experiment, and any assumptions clearly stated. The reason for this is simple, you must be able to make a public statement that can stand up to close scrutiny. The simplest of questions can undo you, such as "so, how do you know this?" The lazy option is of course to rely on 'offsets' rather than change behaviour, but, as discussed earlier, we highly recommend that 'offsets' be used only for those options for which there is no immediate alternative.

Collating an executive summary

Once the project has been selected, there is a real risk of overselling the outcome before you have any real evidence it's going to work over the long-term. Some of these programs will take time. Simply making an intentional statement that you are 'going to be carbon neutral by a certain date' or 'eliminate plastic from our supply chain' does not mean it's possible. A statement could state the intent without committing to a specific outcome until you have some assurance that it will be possible. If you want to make a public statement of intent in the near future or expect the need to address your credentials in your supply chain, then the time to get started is now. You can also hedge your risk by planning several program areas to be funded as available.

The areas that can be dealt with more immediately are internal policy reform such as pay, working conditions, and diversity. There would be a reasonable expectation that any internal reform can meet a public statement in a reasonable timeframe. There is also the area of waste minimisation that is behaviourally based, such as fostering recycling within the production space. These internal programs should be a first order priority to demonstrate intent to support the UN goals.

We all want to get to the good news as soon as possible, but a methodological approach is going to be less risky and more productive in the long term.

Should we prepare for future legislation on sustainability reporting?

We believe the answer is yes. Currently the Australian Government's Clean Energy Regulator has *The Corporate Emissions Reduction Transparency* (CERT) report[55] as a new voluntary initiative for eligible companies to present a snapshot of their climate-related commitments, progress, and net emissions position. That statement is now redundant as the government has passed legislation requiring Climate-related financial disclosure.

We would add that there is increasingly a trend for regulation around corporate transparency. We see for example the US *Corporate Transparency Act 2022* was designed to pursue increased transparency and disclosure of company owners and beneficiaries to combat crimes such as tax evasion, corruption, money laundering, and terrorist financing. This will require millions of companies to disclose their ownership and control structures to the US Treasury. Similarly, the UKs recently passed *Economic Crime (Transparency and Enforcement) Act 2022* seeks to strengthen sanctions enforcement and increase transparency of property and company ownership. The European Union is currently issuing corporate disclosure requirements across the board, especially around beneficial ownership disclosures to curb financial crime and kleptocracy[56]. In the summer of 2021, the European Commission put forward an anti-money laundering package of legislative proposals aimed at strengthening the EU's anti-money laundering and countering terrorism financing rules. There is speculation that this will start to move into social and environmental reporting to protect the interest of shareholders. There are disclosure obligations to the market, but not always sufficient transparency around the claims.

---

[55]The report can be found on the government website of the Clean Energy Regulator. https://www.cleanenergyregulator.gov.au/Infohub/Markets/cert-report

[56]Kleptocracy refers to a society whose leaders make themselves rich and powerful by stealing from the rest of the people.

At the moment in Australia, the focus is on tax evasion and corporate crimes, but that will evolve. Consider the report of the 2006 Australian Parliamentary Inquiry into *Corporate Responsibility - Managing Risk and Creating Value*. Chapter 6 of the Inquiry's findings outlined *Sustainability reporting: background and current status*, and the recommendation of the committee was "that at this time mandatory sustainability reporting was too much of an impost on businesses", so it was maintained as voluntary (recommendation 5). Yet in section 6.44 they did state they were putting the companies on notice:

"The committee also agrees with the view of the Business Roundtable on Sustainable Development that mandating sustainability reporting is an inappropriate response to the current pressures,[236] and notes the view that there may be increasing pressure on the legislature to intervene if companies fail to act."

The current government is also looking for ways to crack down on "greenwashing" and ensuring that Australian firms needed to make credible disclosures to remain competitive in global markets. On the second of March 2023, the ACCC released a report "Greenwashing by Businesses in Australia"[57]. The report outlined the findings of the ACCC's 2022 internet sweep of environmental claims. It details the key issues identified in the sweep and provides an overview of the ACCC's planned work relating to environmental claims and sustainability. Its findings included that overall, 57% of businesses were identified as making concerning claims.

Treasury also has a consultation paper seeking initial views on key considerations for the "design and implementation of the Government's commitment to standardised, internationally-aligned requirements for disclosure of climate-related financial risks and opportunities in Australia"[58]. The government is arguing that business and investors need

---

[57]Australian Competition and Consumer Commission, *Greenwashing by businesses in Australia - Findings of the ACCC's internet sweep of environmental claims.* March 2023

[58]*Climate-related financial disclosure* - Consultation paper dated 12 December 2022 - 17 February 2023. Australian Government - The Treasury

clarity and certainty to manage climate risks and invest in new opportunities. It wants large business and financial institutions to provide more information and greater transparency on how they are responding to climate change and supporting the transition to net zero[59].

We would expect that over time the pressure will be on larger corporation, which will inevitably have a cascading effect on to their small business suppliers.

Global context

Anything you might consider doing in terms of an ESG plan should also consider the global context. Even local actions are likely to be influenced by global events.

The first of those is the climate emergency. Managing continuing climate disasters in a highly populated world takes up a significant level of resources and this is set to increase. Climate change also increases the risk to human health - fire and flood-prone infrastructure, coastal inundation and storms, desertification, all can derail or delay business planning.

The second consideration is still the socio-economic impact of the COVID-19 pandemic. There is no assurance from health experts that the impact of the pandemic is coming to an end. If anything, they are warning of the likelihood of other pandemics given that the conditions that produced the last one still exists. The exact cause of COVID-19 is still uncertain, but corona viruses are zoonotic diseases that transfer across species, and, although rare, could very well happen again anywhere in the world.

The third consideration is the refugee crisis from war and famine that is continuing to increase. At present we have approximately 100 million displaced people. This is an extra burden on economic resources and

---

[59]*More transparency and more investment in cleaner and cheaper energy.* Joint Media statement – The Hon Jim Chalmers MP, The Treasurer, The Hon Chris Bowen MP, Minister for Climate Change and Energy, The Hon Stephen Jones MP, Assistant Treasurer, Minister for Financial Services

that cannot be ignored. It demands emergency attention on top of limited resources. In the meantime, we have an increasing global population, now over eight billion.

The fourth issue is global inflation and its impact on the rising cost of goods and services. Central banks are being very cautious in their response in using interest rate as a lever, but the risk remains. This will impact customer disposable income and is likely to stress businesses in resourcing ESG plans.

Still, given all the above headwinds, global investment is still supportive of the need for ESG and the level of corporate commitment is increasing.

Final comments

Not wanting to end on a negative note, we suggest that there is more opportunity than not in pursuing an ESG plan. It can sometimes be overwhelming, all the issues around us, but we urge you to focus on one or more of the UN targets that is within the capacity of the business you are managing. To be seen to be taking action as part of the community is good for business in a competitive world. Given declining trust in the community over scams, greenwashing, and data breaches, if you do take action be sure it is meaningful and transparent. There is a wide range of avenues that require attention, and any action is better than none. Some issues will demand more immediate action than others, so it's worth engaging your supply chain to look at what can be more easily done. If possible, engage your customers to join you in tackling these issues, whether it is reducing plastic, improving education, protecting wildlife, or reducing emissions. Whatever it is you choose to focus on, if you do it with conviction, this will be the mark of good corporate social responsibility.